Passionate Plots

A Brief Guide to Writing
Erotic Stories and Scenes

Passionate Plots

A Brief Guide to Writing
Erotic Stories and Scenes

Kelly Lawrence

COMPASS BOOKS

Winchester, UK
Washington, USA

First published by Compass Books, 2014
Compass Books is an imprint of John Hunt Publishing Ltd., Laurel House, Station Approach,
Alresford, Hants, SO24 9JH, UK
office1@jhpbooks.net
www.johnhuntpublishing.com
www.compass-books.net

For distributor details and how to order please visit the 'Ordering' section on our website.

Text copyright: Kelly Lawrence 2013

ISBN: 978 1 78279 430 1

A CIP catalogue record for this book is available from the British Library.

Design: Lee Nash

Printed in the USA by Edwards Brothers Malloy

We operate a distinctive and ethical publishing philosophy in all
areas of our business, from our global network of authors to
production and worldwide distribution.

CONTENTS

To struggling writers everywhere: don't give up. Your words make the world a better place.
To the Muse – yes, I am listening, but we really need to talk about these 3am visits.
To Bobby for putting up with being neglected during the writing process. Ditto friends, family and child.

Introduction – Why Erotica?

You would have to have been living in a hole deep underground to miss the recent explosion in popularity of erotic stories and erotic romances. Erotic novels have gone from being discreetly hidden in the far corner of your local bookstore to taking centre stage. In the summer of 2012 chances were that you were either reading the multimillion selling Fifty Shades of Grey trilogy, or talking about it, or listening to people talk about it. The author, E L James, helped open the door to erotica and erotic romances becoming mainstream again, and since Fifty Shades hit the shelves the market has been inundated with new erotic novels and repackaged and re-edited classics. Even mainstream authors have been upping the steam factor in their love scenes in every genre from chick-lit to thriller. In the UK, Black Lace Books have relaunched with a new look, and even traditional romance publishers Mills and Boon brought out 'Spice', a super sexy series where the characters don't necessarily have to live happily ever after (more of this later).

Commercially at least, there has never been a better time to write erotica. So should we all be picking up our pens and frantically scribbling about BDSM, ménage a trois scenarios and dark, brooding lovers with a penchant for kinky sex games?

Well, er, no.

Although, if you intend to write for profit as well as pleasure then you need to be aware of trends, it's never a good idea to write something just because it's in vogue. For example if you're a horror writer specialising in tales of the zombie apocalypse, I doubt you would suddenly turn to romantic comedies just because of the success of the 'Shopaholic' series. So if your talents as a writer tend towards sweet chick-lit or sweeping sagas and you can't even read a love scene without blushing, erotica may not be for you. Ditto if you write in another popular genre and decide to chuck in some erotic scenes when normally your characters never so much as kiss. Remember the old adage 'write what you know'? Personally I prefer 'write what you *love*.'

So how do I know if this genre is for me?

- You enjoy reading erotica and/or romance
- You enjoy writing sensual description
- You're comfortable writing and talking about sex

With regards to the last point, although some past writers of erotica have used pseudonyms for this particular work and kept it relatively quiet, in this day and age authors are expected to promote themselves and engage with their readers, so unless you're planning on only yourself and a few select friends seeing your work you will need to get over any embarrassment pretty quickly. In the run-up to publication of 'Wicked Games', an erotic BDSM memoir, I was featured in the local paper, had to do an interview on BBC radio and even a reading at an erotica night in London. It was all pretty nerve-wracking and blush-inducing, and I love the genre and am proud to be part of it. If you would feel mortified to admit to others that you write erotica or even romance, then you should probably be writing something else.

Perhaps you do write something else, but you want to expand your writing skills and add a level of sensuality to your work. Sex scenes, whether romantic or otherwise, are notoriously difficult to write well, not least because the author feels unsure of how to handle the subject matter. This guide is intended to help all authors craft a sexy sequence that adds to the story. The importance of plot is perhaps most crucial here; after all if you're writing straightforward erotica or erotic romance it follows that the sex is going to be pretty intrinsic to the plot; not necessarily so if you're writing a thriller or American Western and feel it would benefit from added heat. The important thing to keep in mind is that the erotic scene should in some way drive the story forward, whether in terms of character development or the unfolding of the central plot. No matter how well written your erotic scenes, if they're just chucked in any old where they will detract from the story rather than add to it and you risk alienating rather than arousing your reader. If however these scenes are tied in to the plot they can give the whole story that extra oomph. In Chapter One we'll look at some examples of genres and authors that make good use of this.

Personally, I like to write across a variety of genres, but erotic romance is my first love. A good erotic scene will be both evocative and arousing, and this is nowhere more true than in the context of a good romance. I love to explore how two characters physically coming together changes things emotionally and mentally as all good sex should, in my opinion at least. Writing an erotic scene is fun, but also a challenge that I think any aspiring writer should attempt at least once. No matter how fictional the scene, you are to some extent exposing a very private side of yourself and although this can leave you feeling slightly vulnerable, it can make for some very powerful writing.

The aim of this guide then is to share some tips and tricks I've picked up from my own writing experiences, and from other writers, editors and of course readers of erotica and/or erotic romance (we'll get to the differences in the first chapter). I've tried to give an overview of the genre, tips for publication and of course specific advice for all writers for writing those steamy scenes. Perhaps the biggest piece of advice I can give you, and which this whole guide is focused around, is the importance of plot. I'll say it again: an erotic scene, no matter how arousing or well written, should be integral to the story, not just popped in between events in an attempt to spice things up, and in this guide I'll illustrate some ways to achieve this. I'll also be including writing exercises for you to try and a list of resources if you wish to take things further (pun intended).

3

In the first chapter we'll be looking at what erotica is, it's background, history and sub-genres, examples of including sex scenes in other genres, and what you need to think about when you sit down to write your passionate prose. Before we get started, here's a little exercise to get you thinking.

Writing Exercise: How do you define 'erotic'?

Etymologically, the word 'erotic' derives from the Greek erotikos, meaning 'of love'. The World English Dictionary gives its definition as 'concerning or arousing sexual pleasure' and the American Heritage Stedman's Medical Dictionary as 'of or concerning sexual love or desire'. Fairly straightforward, you would think.

Except that sexual desire and arousal is very subjective. Before you attempt to write something erotic to arouse other people, you need to have a sense of exactly what the word 'erotic' means for you. What words, images, situations and sensory experiences do you find arousing?

Take a large sheet of blank paper and write the word 'erotic' in the middle. Create a word web, quickly writing down as many words as come into your mind when you think 'erotic'. Write down whatever springs to mind, be it other words that are particularly evocative for you, a snatch of past memory, even a smell. Don't think too hard, and most definitely don't censor yourself.

When you're done, pick one word or word phrase from your word web as a writing prompt and write for ten minutes. Again, don't think too hard about this, just write. Forget about grammar or structure and just go with it. After ten minutes, put your piece of paper away and look at it a few days later. You may surprise yourself.

Chapter One

What's In A Name?

Porn, erotica, or romance?

Some people use the words 'porn' and 'erotica' interchangeably, and there are really no hard and fast rules. However it's generally accepted that an erotic story will, as well as being sexy, be well written and have a structured plot. A story designated 'pornographic' however is more likely to be just a sex scene or series of sex scenes written purely to titillate, with little or no attention given to story, character or style. 'Porn' is generally seen as a derogatory term when it comes to literature, while certain forms of erotica can be considered very high-brow indeed. Think of Anais Nin's highly explicit yet literary classic 'Delta of Venus' compared to, say, a reader's letter in an adult magazine such as Penthouse.

'Erotic romance' differs from straightforward 'erotica' in that it is, well, romantic. Generally involving two main protagonists who at some point either before or after having amazing sex fall in love and have a happy ending. Erotica on the other hand tends to feature less conventional relationships and may not have a happy ending at all. Erotic romances are currently having something of a hey-day and probably have the most commercial appeal of all these categories, although erotic memoirs are also currently increasingly popular, romantic ending or not.

Although these definitions are generally accepted there is still some overlap, particularly in the media. For example 'Fifty Shades of Grey' is undoubtedly an erotic romance; although it contains very explicit and boundary pushing erotic scenes the couple are deeply in love and have a happy ending, complete with marriage and babies. Yet that didn't stop the trilogy being dubbed, somewhat patronisingly, 'mommy porn' by the tabloids. So although it's a good idea to have an awareness of these definitions, don't get bogged down trying to decide what category your story falls into. If it's well written, it will speak for itself.

Sub-genres

Having said that, there are specific sub-genres within the erotica/erotic romance category that you may want to be aware of, particularly if you're writing to be published. The most typical include

- Historical
- Paranormal
- Contemporary
- Sci-fi/fantasy
- BDSM
- LGBT
- New Adult

Historical erotic stories are, as the name implies, set in a particular historical era. English Regency stories are traditionally very popular at the more romantic end of the market, but an historical can be set way back in the Stone Age or as recently as the Swinging Sixties. With any historical fiction, not just the erotic kind, the setting is almost a character in its own right; the cultural and political mores of the day adding extra depth to the story. This can work excellently for increasing both conflict and opportunities to arouse. For example, if your story is set in an era where people, particularly women, had a lot less sexual freedom than we take for granted now, then that provides boundaries to your main characters getting it on, which provides a point of conflict as well as a tale of forbidden desire, which is always popular. We always want what we can't have, after all.

An important point to remember with historicals is that,

although the history should provide a rich backdrop to the story, it shouldn't swallow it up with reams of information about the particular time and place. If your protagonists are getting hot and heavy in a Roman plaza then some description and background will add texture and drama, but a three page rambling on Roman architecture will not just turn off your reader but probably bore them too.

Paranormals include characters or situations that are outside the realm of ordinary experience. Werewolves or vampires, or haunted houses or fairy glens. As well as giving your imagination free rein, paranormals offer lots of opportunities to up the erotic ante. That dark brooding lover turns out to be a shapeshifter, or the fetish club is actually a hunting ground for a hot vampire…the possibilities are endless.

Contemporary erotica is pretty much the opposite of the two sub-genres I've just mentioned. That is, it's set in the present day and the characters are very much flesh and blood and mortal.

Sci-fi/fantasy involves setting your story in a made-up, alternative world, whether that's another galaxy or an unseen dimension of our world. As with paranormals, sci-fi stories allow for heaps of flexibility within erotic situations and you can really push the envelope. Perhaps your characters live in a world where sex is forbidden, or where open relationships are the norm? This is of course quite a niche category, as with sci-fi in general, but an increasingly popular one.

BDSM stories are particularly popular at the moment in all forms of erotica including romances, memoirs and short stories. BDSM stands for a combination of Bondage, Domination, Submission and Sado-Masochism. There is a lot of variety within this category of course; you could have a romance in which your characters are involved in some spanking and role-play, or an explicit piece of erotica involving a variety of characters, props and scenarios. BDSM stories are usually highly explicit and the best tend to be written by people with at least some hands-on experience.

LGBT involves characters that aren't just heterosexual, and the acronym stands for Lesbian, Gay, Bisexual or Transgendered. As you can imagine there is a huge range of scope within this sub-genre, so much so that some object to the term, but it is still widely used by readers and writers.

New Adult is an attempt to bridge the gap between YA – teenage – and adult fiction, particularly romances, and is a relatively new genre, inspired by the overlap between YA and adult readerships. With huge numbers of adults being fans of the Twilight teenage paranormal series, and hordes of older teenagers getting stuck into the Fifty Shades books, it was noticed that there was a call for books featuring characters aged in their late teens and early twenties, engaging in more explicit erotic scenes than can be found in the YA category. As a result, New Adult fiction is often referred to as 'teen steamies'. Although allowing for more erotic content than YA books this tends to be the least explicit of the genres due to the younger readership, with more of an emphasis on romance.

There is of course a great deal of overlap between sub-genres, with most stories belonging to two or more. For example you may like to write a paranormal New Adult, a historical same-sex romp, or a contemporary BDSM story that features characters of varying sexual persuasions. Plot and sub-genre are often closely intertwined – plot twists that would work in a contemporary setting may be completely unfeasible for a historical story, for example. To get a feel for this and to experiment with which sub-genres feel right for you, try the following writing exercise.

Writing Exercise: What's your Sub-Genre?

Take an idea you may have for a contemporary story and briefly bullet-point the plot. If you can't think of anything right now, choose a story you've recently read. Summarise the main developments in the story. Now choose a historical setting you know something about and 'move' your story into it. How does this change things? Would your characters believably behave in the same way, for example? How would the change of era affect their sexual backgrounds and choices? Make a few notes on how you might need to tweak – or even significantly change – the story.

Now take the same story and imagine one or both of the characters are an otherworldly creature or have some kind of supernatural power. How does this affect the story, do any different possibilities open up? How might this affect their erotic tastes and knowledge?

Do the same thing for any of the other sub-genres you may be interested in. Make your characters same-sex if they were originally heterosexual or vice versa, and consider how this would alter their erotic development. Or for New Adult, make them eighteen and fresh out of college. Perhaps one or both of them are virgins?

Although the point of this exercise is to get a feel for the different sub-genres rather than to produce an actual polished plot, it's worth coming back to your notes at a later date and seeing what ideas they may spark off.

Adding Spice to any Genre

If you're looking to add an erotic element to another genre, the above principles also apply. If you're writing sci-fi for example then the sexier scenes will be very different in flavour than those in a gritty crime thriller. Certain genres lend themselves well to certain styles; many chick-lit titles make good use of tongue-in-cheek, often quite humorous sex scenes, whereas in a horror story, a sex scene may be both gory and quite dark. However a sex scene is not necessarily an erotic one; remember, the definition of 'erotic' is to incite arousal, not to terrify or induce a laughing fit! Of course with time and experience a talented writer might be able to do both, but if you're new to writing erotic scenes, it's best to start with the basics. So you need to honestly consider whether your story would benefit from erotic encounters that are likely to arouse the reader, or whether this would be at odds with the overall theme of the story.

Your work will benefit from more of an erotic element if:

- The central characters have or develop an intimate relationship during the course of the story, and you want to show the physical attraction and emotional development between them.
- You're writing a thriller or suspense story, a highly charged erotic encounter could be the characters natural response to events or feelings, and will add a sense of urgency and passion. Nora Roberts does this well, and crime author Karin Slaughter uses erotic scenes very sparingly, but to tremendous effect.
- You're writing a tale involving loss for example then an erotic and touching encounter can add a sense of poignancy and intimacy.
- Showing a certain character's sexual behaviour will add to the picture you wish to create of them and their character development throughout the story. This is often a device employed in literary fiction (see below).
- You're writing a glitzy Hollywood story of wealth and scandal and erotic scenes would add to the story and the sense of decadence. Think the 'bonkbusters' of Jackie Collins or more recently, Victoria Fox.
- Your story has fantasy, paranormal or sci-fi elements and some added spice would also serve to highlight aspects of the alternative world or unhuman nature of your

characters – for example vampire fiction can be highly erotic in places. Read Anne Rice's 'Blood and Gold' for an excellent example, or Laurell K Hamilton's 'Incubus Dreams'.

- If Historicals are your thing then a well-crafted erotic scene that shows the social mores of the day can give an insight into the characters' motivations and lend authenticity to your story.

Apply the above writing exercise to your current story, exploring how a change of genre will alter how and when you need to include the love scenes.

Literary vs. commercial fiction and erotica

I'm sure you've heard of the distinctions between 'literary' and 'commercial' fiction. Of course, as with the different erotic categories there is some inevitable overlap, but in general terms literary fiction often refers to the more 'serious' type of novel that deals with big, over-riding themes and wins lots of highbrow awards. Commercial fiction, on the other hand, is the mass market paperbacks that you will find in every supermarket, airport, bookshop three-for-two offers and Amazon bestseller lists. Whether it's romance, crime, horror or chick-lit, it tends to be written for the masses and for good reason – it sells. Think of the difference between your more 'serious' musician who writes his own music, plays acoustic guitar and is highly lauded by critics, as opposed to the good looking boy band who frequently storm the charts with their upbeat pop music, and you'll get a rough idea of the distinction. That isn't to say that highly commercial bestsellers can't be incredibly well written – Nora Roberts, for example – or that literary masterpieces don't translate into commercial sales. Last year's literary crime thriller, *Gone Girl* by Gillian Flynn, was hugely popular. But nevertheless the distinction remains, with literary aficionados turning their noses up at commercial writers who write for the market, and popular authors feeling their writing skills aren't being taken seriously.

So what does this mean in terms of erotic writing? The recent surge in erotic novels has tended to focus more on the commercial end of the market, particularly erotic romances such as *Fifty Shades of Grey*, with the predictable literary grumblings being totally at odds with the gazillions of sales. As a generalisation, more literary erotica tends to be quite introspective and have something to say about the human sexual condition, whereas commercial erotica tends to be romantic and more focused on the story itself. Another often heard assumption is that literary erotica – and fiction – tends to be a bit miserable, often drawing some pessimistic conclusions about humanity and society, whereas commercial erotic and romantic fiction wraps things up into a nice happy ending.

Honestly, I prefer happy endings. Certainly within the romance genre. After all if a reader is going to invest their time following a couple's relationship, or one person's sexual journey, it's ultimately always more satisfying to leave them with a warm rosy glow as a reward. That doesn't mean your main characters have to end up pledging their undying love; very popular in today's erotic stories is the notion of a HFN ending – Happy For Now, as opposed to the less realistic happy ever after.

Of course you will most likely find that it's your characters and your plot that drive the ending of your story rather than an attempt to make your tale 'fit' and that's as it should be, but it's always worth bearing in mind where your story fits in among its counterparts, especially if you want to get it out to readers.

A Brief History of Erotic Writing

If we're going to define erotic writing as writing that intends to arouse sexual desire, then this stuff has been around for a long, long time, way before the protagonists in Fifty Shades were even a glint in the author's eye. Erotica has gone in and out of vogue and been pushed underground in certain times and places, but it has existed for as long as storytelling has been around. Sex, after all, is something we all have in common, whatever our particular tastes!

Some of the first erotic writing that we are still aware of today was, believe it or not, penned not between lovers but from worshippers to their ancient gods and goddesses. Before the modern day notion of divinity as a somewhat sexless being and sex itself as decidedly sinful, the gods were portrayed as being as lusty as the rest of us. The verses about the goddess Ishtar and her shepherd lover from ancient Babylon, for example, are both beautiful and positively pornographic. A later version of these even made it into the Bible in the form of the Song of Solomon! Although Old Testament scholars, rabbis and priests have argued that the verse is actually a metaphor for the love between God and Israel, the imagery is undoubtedly highly erotic.

From Ancient Greece we have the poems of Sappho of Lesbos, who wrote such erotic verse dedicated to the goddess Aphrodite that we take the word 'lesbian' from the name of her fabled isle. Prostitutes of the time – who took Aphrodite as their patron goddess – gave us the first recorded accounts of erotic memoirs, writing about their exploits for the entertainment of each other and their patrons. The word 'pornography' is believed to derive from the Greek 'pornographia' which as well as meaning 'writings of prostitutes' was also one of Aphrodite's titles.

Fast forward to the Middle Ages and erotic fiction begins to take shape as a genre, with Boccaccio's *Decameron*, saucy tales about the goings on of priests and nuns, scandalising medieval society in 1351. In fact, the book was being banned right up to 1958! In the 16th century Marguerite de Navarre wrote the *Heptameron*, based on Boccaccio's earlier work, and it was widely read throughout Renaissance Europe.

By the time we reach the Georgian era, when the novel in all forms was becoming increasingly popular, erotic literature was ever more widely read, with Cleland's *Fanny Hill* being published in 1748 and the Marquis de Sade – who of course lent his name to the term 'sadism'- publishing *120 Days of Sodom* towards the end of the period, with graphic scenes of what we now call BDSM.

Erotic fiction went underground during the more puritan Victorian period, but it certainly didn't go away. Writers of erotic literature tended to conceal their identities however and it certainly wasn't spoken about in polite society; attitudes that have prevailed up until perhaps the mid to late twentieth century. DH Lawrence's *Lady Chatterley's Lover*, a tale of infidelity that would seem tame by today's standards, sparked controversy and court cases resulting in a ban on the book under grounds of obscenity. This was in 1928, but by 1978, just fifty years later, we had Anais Nin's now classic erotic work Delta of Venus.

Today, sales of erotic literature are booming, with every genre and style being easily available. If you're serious about writing any genre it's advisable to be well read within it, so here's my personal recommended reading list:

Moll Flanders – Daniel Defoe
Story of O – Pauline Reage
Delta of Venus – Anais Nin
Exit to Eden – Anne Rice
The Dark Garden – Eden Bradley

Chapter Overview

- Although there are no hard and fast rules, 'erotica' differs from 'porn' literature in that there is a focus on story, character and plot, rather than just sex scenes. It's generally also assumed that the quality of writing will be much higher.
- 'Erotic romance' is a blend of erotica and more traditional

romance forms in that the plot contains explicit erotic elements, but these occur in the context of a romance story with a happy ending.

- The main sub-genres within erotic fiction are historical, paranormal, contemporary, sci-fi/fantasy, BDSM, LGBT and the more explicit forms of the emerging New Adult genre.
- A story will often belong to more than one sub-genre, for example a contemporary BDSM story.
- There will be different implications for your plot depending on which genre or sub-genre you choose. Try the writing exercise to experience this for yourself, and as a story prompt.
- When adding an element of erotica to an already established genre, think about what you are trying to achieve, both in terms of your story and the reaction of your reader.
- Commercial erotic fiction often requires a happy ending – at least 'happy for now' – whereas literary erotica is typically more explorative of human sexuality as a whole, and may have less emphasis on a happy ending for the characters.
- Erotic fiction has been around for a very long time – from Biblical times to the repressed Victorian era into the boom of the present day.
- Read within the genre as much as possible to get a 'feel' for it.

In the next chapter I'm going to look at crafting your characters, and the intimate relationships between them.

Chapter Two

The Stars of the Show

The Elements of Characterisation

Who are your story people? Most writing guides or experts will tell you that you need to know your main characters better than you know yourself. Their dreams, their personal foibles, even the name of their childhood imaginary friend. This is never as true as when you're planning on getting your characters all hot and steamy. Before you even plan your erotic scenes you need to know what drives your main characters sexually, what turns them on and turns them off, their deepest darkest desires, how, when, where and to whom they lost their virginity and how they felt about that, any sexual hang-ups or body image issues they may have and how they react when in the throes of orgasm. Writing your sex scenes with all this information firmly in place will make them more authentic and meaningful within the story as a whole, as well as helping you establish the character's emotions and motivations. However, although you need all this information to hand, your reader does not necessarily. Background information on your characters should be revealed gradually, in context, through the characters' thoughts and actions, not through a huge chunk of information by an omniscient narrator (more on viewpoint later). Effective ways of conveying the depth and complexity of your characters include:

- Showing rather than telling
- Interior monologues
- Character quirks and tics
- Dialogue and interactions between characters

Show, don't tell.

Of course, sometimes you just need to tell your reader things. *'Emma was 23 and had worked at the café for three years'* for example, gets the relevant information over much quicker than two pages showing the information by having Emma go to work, giving a description of her place of work, and having her engage in a conversation with her friend about who was number one in the year of her birth. When it comes to those all important details about your character's thoughts, feelings, motivations and goals however, you're much better off showing. It engages the reader, helps them empathise with your character and feel a part of the story. This is perhaps especially important when writing erotic scenes as you want to convey intimacy and evoke arousal. Too much telling will sound dispassionate and detached, leaving the reader feeling they're reading a documentary on the mating habits of humans. Rather, if you want to arouse your reader, you want them to feel every breath and engage with every sensation. Have a look at some of these examples;

'Tom was nervous about the prospect of having sex with Tina.' This is telling, and although it might work in certain parts of the story, this doesn't fit in the middle of a sex scene. Also, unless we're right at the beginning of the story, we likely know that poor Tom is nervous, so we want to feel those nerves, not be told about them. Contrast the first sentence with *'Palms sweaty and his breath catching in his throat, Tom reached out to touch Tina's perfect breasts'*. The clammy palms and bated breath convey the physical sensation of nerves, and the fact that he sees Tina's breasts as perfect shows us he's in awe of her and probably can't believe his luck.

'She had an explosive orgasm, which left her tired' tells us everything we need to know about what has just happened, but nothing about the character's experience. Whereas *'Tina arched her back as wave after wave of pleasure crashed over her, leaving her trembling and heavy-lidded in his arms'* gives us a powerful mental

image and some understanding of how Tina now feels, without once mentioning the words 'orgasm' or 'tired'.

To try this for yourself, take one or all of the following 'telling' sentences and turn them into 'showing' paragraphs.

1. They had slow, satisfying sex before dinner.
2. It was obvious that Tina was much more experienced than Tom.
3. The next morning Tina felt vulnerable.

Interior monologues

You can help your reader 'get to know' your main character by letting them be privy to their thoughts and feelings that they may not be sharing with the other characters in your story. We all have an internal life and often have a running commentary going on inside our heads as we go through our day. So should your characters, unless they are robots. That doesn't mean you need to note every thought that runs through your character's head, as this would be incredibly tedious and time consuming, but glimpses here and there inside a character's head helps them come to life. You can show interior life by directly quoting a thought; *Great,* she thought, fighting not to roll her eyes, *more overtime,* or more subtly simply by changing the focus. For example *'he had a smile on his face'* is an exterior observation, whereas *'he felt full of joy'* gives us an inside look at the character's feelings. It's that simple.

When writing love scenes, a glimpse into at least one character's inner life is crucial. If we come back to Tom and Tina in the exercise above, we can see how interior thought gives us more insight into Tom's nerves and Tina's vulnerability. We could add the following to our showing sentences:

He couldn't help thinking how out of his league she was. What on earth did she see in him? But then Tina tipped her head back and moaned, pushing all such thoughts to the back of Tom's mind. In this sentence we get a telling glimpse into Tom's thoughts, before coming back to the exterior in order to keep the story moving and the focus of the scene on the erotic. This hint of Tom's insecurity can foreshadow a later conflict.

Before she drifted into sleep Tina wondered how this would affect things in the morning. She knew, without a doubt, that everything would be changed. This peek into Tina's post-coital thoughts lets us see how she has been affected and sets the scene for her vulnerable feelings the morning after, as well as indicating that the scene we have just read was not just an erotic interlude but a pivotal turning point.

Character quirks and tics.
You make your character individual by giving them individual characteristics. A tendency to roll their eyes, bite their nails, or the fact that they hate potatoes or love the smell of engine oil. Dropping these little nuggets of information helps the reader build up a fully dimensional picture of the character. The trick is to give them traits that are lovable rather than annoying. To use an example from Fifty Shades again, Ana's constant biting of her lip every time she is aroused starts to grate on me after the first 100 pages, whereas Helen Fielding's Bridget Jones has a habit of using the occasional French word to try and sound sophisticated – though she is anything but – which I find adorable. Perhaps the trick is to use such things sparingly.

When it comes to erotic scenes, giving your story people individual sexual characteristics can help the scenes come alive. One character may love to play jazz music when making love for example, while another may love being softly bitten on the back of the neck, a fact the lover uses to good advantage. Ensure that whatever characteristics you choose, they are actually sexy. A character with a tendency to break wind in bed or wear holey socks isn't going to do anything for your heat levels.

Physical characteristics can stick in your reader's mind also, long after other details have been forgotten. Long, white fingers, a dimple in a chin, freckles across the top of cheekbones or a scar below a hipbone; these little details help distinguish your character and can be used to excellent effect in erotic scenes:

The sight of those slim white fingers with her scarlet nails caressing his shaft made him gasp. Musician's fingers, *he thought before she picked up her rhythm and he ceased to think, only feel.*

She laid a burning trail of butterfly kisses down the side of his body, pausing at the crescent shaped scar below his hipbone and nibbling the taut flesh, then pressing her lips to it as if the action could erase both the scar and its accompanying memories.

To try this yourself take a character of your own, give them a distinguishing feature and write a short erotic scene which highlights it.

Dialogue and interactions.
How your character talks reveals a lot about them. Their interactions with each other are what create your story and often, shape your character.

Dialogue is the ultimate way to show rather than tell. You can get across, in a short conversation, reams of information that would take you two pages to describe. Your characters need voice; and it is often this that draws the reader in.

How do you apply this to erotic sequences? Well, sex is perhaps the ultimate interaction between two people, and as we've discussed the best erotic scenes are those that add to character development and to the main thrust of the story. Sex changes things between people; even if it is the most casual of hook-ups any further interaction between the two characters will be inevitably altered.

The dialogue between your lovers can add to the erotic element, or illustrate the emotions each character is experiencing, or both. It can be tricky to get right though. In real-life, plenty of couples don't really talk during sex, apart from perhaps the odd 'left a bit' and it may be more in keeping with your story people's natures to stay quiet. But they are bound to talk at some point, whether just before or after, and what they say and how they say it can tell the reader volumes about them, as well as hint at what's going to happen next. If after sex for example one character is suddenly terse or taciturn, we know there's trouble ahead. If they have an intimate conversation and reveal secrets about themselves, we know that the sex has brought them closer together.

Dialogue should show what's going on inside the character; for example in my New Adult romance the heroine, Ashley, is breathless and a bit stammery when she's on the verge of having sex for the first time. So we know she's both nervous and excited without her having to say 'by the way, I'm nervous and excited'. Nervous Tom from our previous exercise could blurt out 'you're so beautiful' as he touches Tina, illustrating his awe for her and intense attraction to her.

How about dialogue during sex? Like I said, there often isn't any, but it might be in keeping with your characters, as well as being highly erotic for the reader, for them to engage in some 'dirty talk'. I'd advise a light touch, and don't suddenly change how the characters usually talk; if they never swear and in fact find it repellent then they're unlikely to start shouting 'fuck me' at the top of their voice. But if you think that's exactly what your feisty, slightly potty-mouthed heroine would do, then let her do it. Dirty talk is often used to great effect in BDSM themed scenes to illustrate one partner's sexual dominance over the other; a well-timed 'yes sir' for example.

Heroes and heroines

As writers, we're constantly aware of the need to make our characters feel like real living people. We want to hear them breathing on the page. So avoiding stereotypical cardboard cutout characterisation is a must. That isn't made very easy by the fact that certain genres – and genre readers – will have very clear unwritten formulas for the main characters. You can try to avoid these all you want but the truth is, if you're writing commercial fiction you need to give readers a little of what they want. Without making your characters seem two dimensional. Not easy, huh?

Within the romance genre, or any storyline that has romantic interaction between the main characters, you're going to come up against the alpha male hero – who often has a troubled past that can only be redeemed by the love of a good woman – and his counterpart, the feisty independent heroine who secretly yearns for the love of a good strong man. Even in a less conventional LGBT romance where the characters aren't the usual male-female pairing, or a sci-fi story where they may not even be human, you will still find variations on these blueprints. One character will have definite alpha hero traits which the other will suitably swoon over – while of course, remaining feisty and independent.

As writers we may roll our eyes at this, but the fact is that readers have certain expectations of particular genres that we would be wise to fulfil. After all, as a reader of erotic romance when I curl up with a new book I fully expect my alpha male to strut onto the page, ruggedly handsome and with testosterone oozing from every pore. This guy doesn't just show up in romances either, but is a regular feature of thrillers, crime novels and action adventure stories, and not just those written by women either; check out Lee Child's series of novels featuring Jack Reacher.

Having said this, I'm not advising you to take your interesting and unconventional characters and turn them into Ken and Barbie. You know your story, you know your characters – especially if you've followed the advice in this chapter – and you know what fits and what doesn't. It's just always a good idea to be aware of these things as they provide you with a platform from which to work. Even if your story turns conventional tropes on their heads, you need to know what they are in the first place. There's also a very good reason why these character traits work so well in a romantic and/or sexual scenario. They're sexy. The dynamic interplay between opposites, male and female, yin and yang, submissive and dominant, make for sizzling sexual tension that if used effectively can really ramp up the tension in your story and propel it forward. Think about your characters and how their coming together creates this interplay, and how this is going to affect their behaviour in the bedroom, and subsequently out of it. Perhaps the quiet, reclusive mystery detective finds his manly side unleashed by uninhibited sex with a female suspect, which then leads to him developing greater confidence in himself and his abilities and helping to solve the case? Or you can turn the stereotypes on their head by, for example, having a typical alpha hero reveal his secret love of being dominated in BDSM scenes with the quiet librarian who has a secret identity as a professional dominatrix. What really matters is that your erotic scenes reveal that dynamic interplay between your characters that put the 'sex' in sexual tension.

Another reason to be aware of stereotypical expectations is that if you're not, you could find they creep into your writing without your meaning them to, simply because, regardless of our own sexual tastes or even those of our characters, the typical male/female dominant/submissive mix is the natural default scenario for most of us, thanks to cultural conditioning and, dare I say it, evolutionary impulses. As a result your otherwise complicated and well-rounded characters could turn into Fred and Wilma Flintstone as soon as they reach the bedroom with no reason or bearing on the story. This won't arouse your readers, it will just baffle them. If you want your characters to show very different sides of themselves when in between the sheets, you need to make this clear that this is what you're doing (but do remember to show rather than tell).

A popular theme in much recent erotica and erotic romance is that of the submissive female, again partly due to the success of the Fifty Shades trilogy and BDSM erotica in general. There's nothing wrong with this – my own book 'Wicked Games' explores this theme – and it's a popular sexual fantasy but please, don't make your heroine 'too stupid to live'. However submissive and willing she may be sexually, please don't make her a drip or have a victim complex when she puts her clothes back on. Although characters of this nature can feature in stories of various genres – particularly slasher stories, where they usually get killed pretty early on – they are rarely the main protagonist, simply because the reader will likely be thoroughly annoyed by them. Two obvious examples are Ana from Fifty Shades who, even though she is an attractive woman in her twenties living in New York, is still a virgin – who has never even masturbated – and yet signs a contract allowing Mr Grey to dominate her in every area of her life; and Bella from Twilight who comes across as a complete drip until Edward finally turns her into a vampire. If you do want your female character to, at least initially, be a bit of a wet blanket or ridiculously sexually naïve then at least give the reader some background as to why they are this way, and have them face their issues as we move through the story. We can all relate to characters that have weaknesses and insecurities and are even a bit foolish at times, but if your reader is shouting 'you idiot!' at your heroine as they are reading then it's not a good sign. Of course there are plenty of male characters who can inspire this reaction too, but the current trend seems to all too often leave us with female protagonists who have all of the backbone of a limp lettuce. Readers want characters they can empathise with, but also aspire to be.

Ultimately, your erotic scenes should reveal things about the characters, ramp up tension between them and have an impact on their motivations within the story. And be sexy.

Is three always a crowd?

Should your sex scenes only ever contain two people? Well it rather depends on what you're writing. If it's a romance – or the characters are having a romance within the context of the story – then yes. Mostly. In 'Wicked Games' the two main protagonists have a brief erotic scene with another important character. Although this interlude is written to be arousing, it also serves as a pivotal turning point in the couple's relationship. So there is room for manoeuvre here, but don't overcomplicate things and lose focus on the central characters and plot.

Certain genres and stories do lend themselves to erotic encounters involving more than one person, for example stories set in other worlds where sexual conventions may be very different, or paranormal stories where the otherworldly creatures have very different views about sexuality. Laurell K Hamilton's paranormal books do this very well, with scenes involving group sex between fairies, elves, werewolves and vampires that somehow manage to be powerfully evocative yet not at all sleazy. Erotica as a genre naturally lends itself to themes of sexual explo-ration, and having your main character take part in a threesome or moresome could be a powerful way of furthering your character's development. An initial encounter may lead your character to become involved in the world of swinging, or question their sexuality and start to explore same sex relationships.

Other scenarios which lend themselves to erotic encounters between more than two people are your main character/s exploring the world of Tantra, or attending sex therapy, or becoming involved in the sex, drugs and rock and roll lifestyle. Certain historical periods are famed for their debauchery and decadence so even an historical romp may feature the occasional threesome or even orgy. If it fits and furthers your plot, go for it. If you're new to writing erotic scenes however, it's probably a good idea to start with the basics! Also bear your target audience in mind; you want to arouse, not shock.

Using Viewpoint to Convey Character

There are different viewpoints you can use to write your story, and each will have a different impact on your sexy sequences.

First-person.

You write the story from the viewpoint of your main character, in 'I' form. Writing in this way allows the reader to immediately feel intimate with the protagonist, but it does mean the whole narrative is told through their eyes. You can't see events from anyone else's point of view or know anything that the narrator doesn't. With erotic scenes, although it limits the 'view' it allows us to really experience things with the character, almost as if we're experiencing it ourselves, and so can be highly arousing.

Unreliable narrator.

This is as above, except that for some reason the narrator can't directly tell us the whole story, or we are told a skewed version of events. This may be because the narrator has a limited viewpoint – perhaps he or she is a child – has skewed perceptions due to mental health difficulties or cultural conditioning, or is quite simply lying. This often gets revealed gradually through the story, with the reader having to glimpse between the lines to find out what is really going on. This viewpoint is used to chilling effect in Gillian Flynn's *Gone Girl*. It is not however something I would recommend if you're writing a sexy story, as it can be confusing and even disturbing.

Third-person subjective.

Written in the third-person 'he said, she said' but from a particular character's point of view: *the smell of the farm reminded him of home, and he felt instantly nostalgic. Dad would love it here,* for example. This viewpoint can change during the course of the story (not advisable within a short story) and is often employed in romances to show both protagonists view of events. Don't constantly jump from one viewpoint to another within the same scene – known as 'head-hopping' – as this can be confusing and the reader will feel like they or you have multiple personality disorder. This viewpoint works for all genres and is the most common, so it's perfect for your erotic scenes.

Third-person omniscient.
Written objectively, with no forays inside the character's heads. Very much telling rather than showing. It went out of fashion with the classics, mainly because it makes it almost impossible to engage with the characters, although literary short stories may make good use of this viewpoint. It certainly isn't very erotic. However in any third-person story there is usually a touch of the omniscient mingled with the more prevalent subjective viewpoint, simply as a way to quickly convey basic information. *It was a Sunday morning,* for example.

Narrator at a distance.
Although this is essentially the first person, it feels like the third person omniscient. The story is narrated by a fictional character who is 'watching' the events of the story unfold, and has a minimal amount of interaction with the main characters. John le Carré makes good use of this in some of his spy novels, though personally I find it prevents any engagement with the story. I certainly wouldn't advise it as a viewpoint for an erotic scene, unless you're planning on writing for a very specific market of sexual voyeurs.

Second person.
This makes you the main character, who the story is happening to. As you can imagine, it's rarely used, though there is a market in those types of adventure books that allow you to choose what happens next and has a variety of different endings. I don't think there's ever been an erotic scene written in this way, and probably

for very good reason. Having said that, if you're feeling experimental it may work for a short flash-fiction piece, but I would recommend you don't try this as a beginner.

Your viable choices of viewpoint here are probably first-person and third-person subjective (with a touch of the omniscient) so let's have a look at the pros and cons of each in terms of your erotic writing.

First-person
Pros
- Gives the reader extra empathy with the main character
- Allows the reader to experience the character's sensations and feelings at first-hand
- Puts the reader in the shoes of the protagonist – can be highly arousing when reading an erotic scene

Cons
- You're restricted to one viewpoint
- The reader can never know anything about the story that the narrator doesn't

Third-person
Pros
- You can reveal whatever you want to the reader, as the narrative voice doesn't have to be restricted to the location and perception of the main protagonist.
- When it comes to the love scenes you can show the feelings and sensations of both lovers, which many readers prefer.

Cons
- If your story has one main protagonist you lose intimacy with them, as you're always one step removed.

Writing Exercise: Lonely Hearts

It's time to get to know your main character/s – intimately.

Take your main character – or your hero and heroine, if it's a romance – and write a dating advert for them. I don't mean a three sentence ad of the type you might find in the newspapers, but the kind of lengthy profile you will find on dating websites that go into great detail about the person and what they want from a relationship. Some even have in-depth psychological questionnaires. Try writing one of these – or even filling out an online profile, but make sure it doesn't go live – as if you were your character. If your story is highly erotic you might like to have a look at some of the saucier dating websites and write an ad for your character based on finding a sex partner rather than a romantic relationship. This will help you get inside your character's head and think about things you might have missed. It can be a lot of fun too, but don't get so distracted on dating websites that you don't write your story!

If you don't want to or can't check out dating sites on the internet, here are a few examples of the questions you might get asked when filling out a profile, from the sweet to the saucy. Answer the questions as if you were the character and then write your ad.

1. Where would you go and what would you do on the ideal first date?
2. What are the five most important characteristics in a potential partner?
3. Do you have or want children? If not, why not?
4. Where do you see yourself in five years time? Or ten?
5. Describe your most memorable sexual encounter.
6. Where would be your ideal holiday location and why?
7. If you could be any character in a novel or film, who would it be and why?
8. What are your five worst turn-offs in a potential partner?
9. What is your biggest sexual fantasy?

As well as getting you up close and personal with your character, you can use the ad as a story prompt; perhaps the character in question does try using these sites, leading to erotic encounters.

Chapter Overview

- You should know your main characters inside out, but you don't need to share all of this information directly with the reader.
- As much as is practical when writing erotic scenes 'show' rather than 'tell' the reader what's happening and how the person is experiencing it. Have a go at some of the examples given.
- Give your main characters an inner life: thoughts, feelings and perceptions, or they will seem like robots.
- Giving your characters little quirks and distinguishing features will breathe life into them.
- Small, seemingly unimportant physical characteristics can help paint an intimate picture within a love scene.
- Your characters come alive when they interact and speak with each other.
- Dialogue is an efficient way to show rather than tell.
- Any dialogue during an erotic encounter should be in keeping with how the character usually talks.
- Use 'dirty talk' sparingly for a powerful effect.
- Traditional stereotypes often dominate characters in romantic situations, especially the 'alpha male'.
- Genre readers will have particular expectations of the main characters.
- It's fine to play around with traditional stereotypes and even turn them on their head; but do be aware they exist, or they could creep into your writing unbidden.
- Sexually submissive females are currently popular in erotic writing, but do note that the word is 'submissive' not 'stupid'.

- Erotic scenes involving more than two people can work, but be careful if the main characters are involved in a romance.
- Scenarios and stories that can work well for three or moresomes include BDSM, sci-fi, paranormal, themes of sexual exploration, Hollywood style 'bonkbusters' and even some particularly decadent historical periods.
- Different viewpoints you can choose include first-person, which includes an unreliable narrator, third-person subjective, third-person omniscient, narrator at distance, and second-person. Those most likely to work for erotic scenes are third-person subjective and first-person.
- Use the writing exercise to get a clear idea of your character's sexual and/or romantic desires.

In the next chapter we're going to look at those essential ingredients for any good story: drama and conflict, and how to use your erotic scenes to increase these. We'll also talk about how to convey and increase a particular source of conflict: sexual tension.

Chapter Three

Drama and Conflict

Why conflict is essential to your plot

Your story needs conflict. Even if you want to write a whimsical, light-hearted country saga there needs to be some conflict, even if it's just a question of who stole Farmer Giles' potatoes. The reasons are fairly obvious. Without conflict

- Your story has nowhere to go and the reader will lose interest.
- Your characters don't develop and change and the reader will lose interest.
- The story doesn't feel 'important' and the reader will lose interest...
- With no conflict to resolve, there's no climactic ending; although the reader will never get there anyway, as they lost interest at chapter four!

I'm sure you get my point. Think of any story you like, and it's the conflict that drives the plot and informs the motives of the characters. In romances there is often conflict between the soon-to-be lovers. In literary erotica, the conflict may be between the protagonist's secret sexual desires and society's expectations. On a larger scale, the conflict in a political thriller could be a world war. Big or small, there needs to be conflict.

There are roughly three types of conflict

- Intrapersonal
- Interpersonal
- External

All of these may be present within the same story, feeding into each other and creating a multi-layered story.

Intrapersonal conflict.
This is essentially conflict within the self. Addictions for example, or mental health issues, or a sense of duty warring with an intrinsic need for freedom, or perhaps an ex-cult member struggling to overcome ingrained thought patterns. Everyone experiences this to some degree. Self-doubt, body image issues and berating yourself for doing what you want to do rather than what you should do are all forms of milder intrapersonal conflict. Your main characters, unless they're saints or sociopaths, are going to have some degree of intrapersonal conflict going on in relation to the conflicts outside themselves. A typical theme in romance is the commitment-phobe struggling with feelings of love, and in erotica the conflict between 'being good' and wanting to be 'dirty'. Or the super successful rock star hiding a cocaine addiction, the jaded detective who drinks too much, or the gorgeous model who in fact suffers from body dysmorphic disorder.

Interpersonal conflict.
This is conflict between characters. In the above examples for instance, the commitment-phobe finds themselves arguing with the love interest, the sexual explorer has issues with her family who threaten to disown her and the rock star may be engaged in a vicious royalty battle with a band member, or be in danger from a disgruntled drug dealer. The detective is hunting a vicious terrorist who targets the detective with taunting messages, making it personal, and the model alienates all her friends by acting like a complete cow and is in murderous rivalry with another model. Unfortunately we humans are an argumentative lot, so your options for interpersonal conflict are endless.

External conflict.

As the name implies, the conflict comes from 'outside'. The government perhaps, a war, or even nature in the form of an earthquake or impending Ice Age. Quite often these 'big conflicts' spur the characters on to overcoming their internal conflicts and tapping into strengths they didn't know they had. To again use the above examples: perhaps the commitment-phobe finds out his disgruntled lover is in the path of a tornado and rushes off to save her, revealing his love when he does so. The newly liberated sexual adventurer finds her freedom curtailed when right-wing fanatics take over the country and the rock star, thanks to his dodgy drug habit, finds himself caught up in a gangland war. The detective is fighting against time to track down and disarm a terrorist threat, and the model finds herself at the head of a campaign calling for the banning of size zero models.

Where does sex fit into all of this? Conflict provides tension, danger and character motivation, all of which can give rise to erotically charged moments. Just remember, they must fit in with and further the plot. Sticking with our conflicted characters, the romance with the commitment phobe and the story of the woman fighting for her sexual freedom offers lots of scope for integral erotic scenes, but what about the rest? These are genres which don't always require erotic scenes, and as a result you need to take extra care that your characters' sexual encounters are adding to the story, not detracting from it. Perhaps the rock star finds himself powerfully attracted to the drug dealer's girlfriend, sparking off an affair that exacerbates the conflict. The detective finds himself forced to hide out in a bomb shelter with the ex he never got over, and the fear of impending death has them falling into each other's arms. Or the model starts a relationship with a blind guy who doesn't care what she looks like, giving rise to some touching erotic scenes as well as furthering her character development.

Ultimately sex is a huge part of life and so are relationships so every genre has room for erotic content, providing it's well written and makes sense in context of the plot (that word again…we'll get to it in the next chapter).

Creating Drama

Drama is what happens as a result of the conflict. Sooner or later the conflict builds to boiling point, and then the big drama begins. Prior to this there will probably be lots of mini-dramas that add to the rising tension. Your erotic scenes may be mini-dramas in themselves; if you're writing erotica, they will probably be the big drama and part of the climax too (pun intended!).

So what exactly is 'drama'? Well, let's say you've got your main characters, a vampiress and a soldier. They have their intrapersonal conflicts – she is struggling not to drink human blood, he has insomnia – as well as conflicts with other people – she with her vampire maker, he in a vicious custody battle with his ex-wife – and initially they hate each other too. The external conflict could be an impending war between the vampire clan and the military due to a new government bill making it illegal to drink human blood. So you've got your characters, and your conflict. When all this comes together and something significant happens, there's your drama. To give a brief example: the soldier and vampiress meet and he, suffering from lack of sleep, mistakes her for a known blood-drinker. They fight, and she gets away. There's your first dramatic scene, and you've introduced new conflict and hopefully mentioned the fact that they can't help finding each other attractive; so now you've set the scene for later erotic encounters too. The story continues until you get to the big dramatic scene: a showdown with the master vampire in which she nearly dies and has to drink blood to stay alive. The aftermath – and resolution – of this is a new agreement between the government and the vampire clan, and a happy romantic ending for the two protagonists. Easy huh? Now it's time for you to have a go…

Writing Exercise: Creating Conflict and Drama

Pick any two characters out of the following list. Don't think about it too hard; just pick the first two you like.

1. A right-wing female politician
2. A werewolf
3. A vegan
4. A Mormon woman, a second wife in an arranged poly-amorous marriage
5. A male tarot card reader
6. A fallen angel who is trying to get his wings back
7. A fifteenth century courtesan
8. A dairy farmer
9. An assassin
10. A customs officer

Now pick one conflict from each of the following lists.

Intrapersonal
1. An eating disorder
2. Agoraphobia – fear of wide open spaces
3. Compulsive gambling
4. Perfectionism
5. A problem with authority

Interpersonal
1. Divorce
2. Sibling rivalry
3. A work colleague that always tries to sabotage a character's projects
4. A mysterious stalker is threatening one of the characters
5. Vicious arguments with the neighbours

External
1. A war between humans and aliens
2. A comet is about to hit Earth
3. Economic recession
4. A plane crash
5. An outbreak of a deadly virus

Put your characters and your conflicts together and see what happens. What dramas could arise? Where is there potential for erotic moments and tension and how does this feed the plot? What genre is this story? What happens in the 'big drama' and how is the conflict resolved?

Have fun with this, it's not a test, but a playful exercise designed to get your creative juices going. If you enjoy it, start again and pick different characters and conflicts and see where they take you. Well done – you've just structured a basic plot! We'll come back to these principles in more detail in chapter four, with an emphasis on plotting your sex scenes, but for now I want to look at a specific source of conflict that has particular bearing on learning to craft believable erotic sequences. That all important sexual tension.

Sexual Tension 101

What is sexual tension? It's that simmering between two people who are attracted to each other but are fighting it, or can't be together for whatever reason, or the first time you talk to someone and you look at each other and just know you're going to end up between the sheets, but you've only just met and you're in public/company so it wouldn't be polite to say anything. If the couple becomes long-term, sexual tension evolves into chemistry, where you're finishing each other's sentences and even your friends sense the simmering heat between you.

Sexual tension is crucial for your story if you're writing an erotic romance or erotica; think of it as foreplay. In these genres sexual tension will be one of if not the major source of conflict. It sounds like an obvious point, but I've read a few erotica novels where, although the sex scenes come fast and furious, there's little or no sexual tension, which results in the reader not really caring about the characters or even what happens next, flicking through to the sex scenes and discarding the book.

Even if you're writing in another genre, if you're planning on including an erotic scene, it's still important to have some levels of sexual tension that give the reader a build-up. Otherwise the sex scenes appear to come out of nowhere and can jar the reader out of the story. Sexual tension serves to give the reader a hint at the scenes to come, so by the time they reach the first love scene they'll be not just expecting it but looking forward to it. It can also serve your plot in other ways; a little sexual tension simmering away can work with other points of conflict in the story to up the overall rising tension and drama. Particularly in thrillers and action-adventure novels, two characters battling outside conflict while sexual tension simmers away between them really adds to the levels of excitement and urgency. Just look at some Hollywood films for examples of this. The same principle can work in horrors and Westerns too. Historical fiction can also benefit from a good dollop of sexual tension and done well it can really add to the plot; think of the restrained and corseted Victorian era with all that passion bubbling under the surface for example.

Of course sexual tension is subtle and hard to describe; like that all elusive chemistry, you know when it's there but it's almost impossible to pin down and define. Therefore, although our stories might need this form of tension, it's not the easiest thing to convey in words, unlike a film where you can practically see the sparks fly between characters. Here is where you really need to be able to 'show not tell'. Telling your readers there's sexual tension between your characters, even in the first-person, won't let them feel it. So how do you do it? The best novels have noticeable levels of rising tension that seem to have emerged naturally between the characters without the author's input; this may be the case (sometimes in the flow of writing you lose yourself in the characters and only afterwards realise the complexities and subtleties in the writing) but the majority of the time the effect is one that the author intended. There are a few ways you can show sexual tension between the characters:

- Dialogue (banter, innuendo and subtext)
- Body language
- Awareness of each other's physical attributes
- Sensual details

Dialogue
The use of banter between two characters trying to fight or avoid their attraction to each other is a strong device in romance novels, and if this is an area you're not familiar with I suggest you read a few and see how other writers do it. 'Banter' can be used to refer to flirting, teasing, even a heated debate if it's already been made clear the characters would rather be ripping off the other's clothes than their head. Whatever the context, banter is witty, fast-paced dialogue with a sexual edge. You can make this sexual aspect quite clear with the use of flirting or innuendo, or subtle with the use of subtext.

How do your characters flirt? Think about their personalities and don't make your heroine turn into a pouty-lipped giggling hair flicker if she's usually quiet and serious, or a ballsy no-nonsense kind of gal, or your down-to-earth guy metamorphoses into Mr Charmer. Let your characters lead.

Sexual tension between characters often arises due to some interpersonal conflict between them. This may be because of the situation they're in, one a cop, the other a fugitive, to give an obvious example much beloved of Hollywood screenwriters, but is at its most effective when there is a conflict between their personality types. As we all know, opposites attract. If for example one character is naturally flirtatious while the other finds them frivolous – but is secretly enjoying their attentions – you've set the scene for some witty, sexy repartee that will positively have the pages smoking. Especially if the more flirtatious character then begins to up the ante on purpose in order to get a rise out of the other. Just don't keep this going on indefinitely or the bantering soon begins to read like bickering, and this isn't sexy.

Innuendo is a great way of injecting an element of simmering sexual attraction into a conversation without the characters blatantly saying 'I really fancy you.' An innuendo is a phrase that means something completely ordinary in the context of the conversation, but can also be taken as implying something else – usually sexual. It can be used deliberately as in the example above to get a rise out of the other character, or you could have your story person say something suggestive without meaning to, only realising from the surprised or interested reaction.

The only thing to be careful of is that your dialogue doesn't become too obvious, with your innuendoes becoming blatantly sexual in a 1970's skin flick kind of way. No 'gun in the pocket' jokes, please.

Sub-text is a subtler way to show tension of any kind in dialogue – it's the reading between the lines, what the characters don't say – and it only works in the context of what has gone before. For example, look at this simple exchange:

John 'I've always liked to dance.'
Jane 'I remember.'

This could mean anything. John and Jane could be old friends having a casual conversation at a school reunion, with no further implications. However if we already know that John and Jane are old flames that are still attracted to each other, and that this is the first time they've seen each other since a brief night at a friend's wedding where John asked Jane for dance that turned steamy and ended up with him sweeping her out of the ballroom onto a balcony for a passionate embrace, then the exchange takes on a different meaning. We know they are now both thinking of that last frenzied embrace, and that the tension is growing between them. What isn't said can be as powerful as what is.

Body Language

It may seem strange to talk about body language in a story, but sometimes a simple mention of one character leaning towards the other, or biting their lip, can convey unspoken attraction and tension. Body language gives a lot away about us and often reveals our feelings towards another person regardless of what we're saying. In a way body language is a subtext in itself. But of course our readers can't see our characters, so a hint here and there adds to the overall picture you're trying to build. For example, we can add this to our exchange above, making the subtext clearer.

'I've always liked to dance,' he said, the corner of his mouth moving upwards with the hint of a smile. Jane took a step closer, looking up at him from under her eyelashes.

'I remember,' she said.

Of course, you don't need to give the reader a running commentary of every shift of position or raised eyebrow, and if you're going for witty banter then keep the dialogue fast and pacy without much prose in between, but used lightly a visual picture of the character's body language can illustrate the attraction between them.

Awareness of each other's physical attributes

It's fine every now and then to blatantly mention one character's notice of the other. It helps the reader see through the character's eyes and get a sense of their desire. As with the body language use sparingly, as you don't want your story people to be constantly leering over each other, but there's no reason why a heroine can't catch herself appraising the broad shoulders of the hero as he walks away from her. Or his eyes can't briefly follow the sway of her hips.

Sensual details.

Sex and desire are communicated through the body and the senses. In Chapter Five we'll look at using the five senses to add description to your sex scenes, but while your characters are still building up to getting tangled in the sheets you can evoke your readers' senses by briefly mentioning smells and tastes, how deep his voice is, or the little dimple in her cheek when she smiles. Raised goose bumps after the briefest of touches on the arm…

Writing Exercise: Adding Sexual Tension

Take the simple dialogue below and add to it using the techniques above to give a sense of sexual tension and desire. Play around with it trying one technique, then another, or a combination, until you feel the exchange crackles with chemistry.

> Jane. 'John. It's been quite a while.'
> John. 'Indeed. Four…five years?'
> Jane. 'More like eight, actually. It was at Gina's birthday party.'
> John. 'Oh yeah. Gina. I remember you wearing a red dress.'

Another way to add sexual tension and conflict is to keep your characters apart. Don't let them get each other straight into bed, and once they have, find a twist to keep them apart, sexually if not physically. Even if your romance/sexual encounter is a sub-plot as part of your thriller or family saga or sci-fi novel rather than the main thrust of your story, keeping the sexual tension going will add impetus to the main conflict.

Chapter Overview

- Conflict is essential to your story to develop your plot and your characters.
- Intrapersonal conflict is conflict that arises within the self.
- Interpersonal conflict is conflict with a specific person or group of people.
- External conflict is conflict with an outside force: terrorism, culture, even Nature.
- In most stories a combination of these will be present and will affect each other.
- Drama is what happens as a result of the conflict. When your conflict reaches boiling point – most effectively at the end of your story – the 'big drama' or climax will occur. Play around with the writing exercise to see the effect conflict can have on your characters and how this affects the erotic elements of the story.
- Your sex scenes can in themselves be the dramatic moments, and sexual tension is both a good source of conflict and helps 'build' the reader towards the erotic scenes.
- You can show sexual tension through dialogue with the use of banter, innuendo and subtext.
- Other ways to convey sexual tension include body language, awareness of each other's physicality, and sensual detail. Try these for yourself using the exercise given.

So you've got your characters, and you know the challenges that await them and how to up the tension levels. Now we need to weave it all together, and ensure that your erotic scenes are adding to and enhancing your story.

Chapter Four

Plot, Plot, Plot

Planning and plotting; your story arc

I've been stressing the importance of plot all the way through this guide, but what exactly is it and how do we do it? Your plot is, at its most basic, your plan for what happens in your story.

You start with an idea or a character for a particular story. If you've been using the exercises in sequential order for a new story then you'll know what genre you're writing in, have got to know your main characters and have an idea of the challenges that face them and the dramas that are going to arise. Putting that all together into a tight framework is your plot.

It's not however as simple as making notes on what happens in which chapter, though of course that's the basis of it. You need to know what's driving your story. What is your protagonist's main goal and motivation? What is the Big Question of your story that will be resolved at the end? All stories have a big question, whether it's as simple as 'will she marry him' or 'will she manage to find and dismantle the bomb and save the world.' These are what drive your story and create a gripping, pacy plot, whatever genre you're writing in, that will keep your reader interested to the end and thinking about your story long after they've closed the final pages.

Your 'story arc' refers to the development and growth of your plot. As your story progresses there should be a clear rising of tension and a picking up of pace towards the inevitable climax. Your main characters also need to go on a journey that reflects this, developing and growing as the plot unfolds. This is often referred to as the character's individual story arc, or their 'character arc'.

Whole books have been written on plotting and story arcs,

but for the purposes of this guide we're going to focus on plotting the erotic elements of your story to ensure they fit in and add to your story arc and the character development of your main protagonists. First though, let's take a look at just exactly how you get down to planning your story.

Most writers fall broadly into one of two camps: those who get a basic idea or a fully formed character and sit down to write with no real idea of how the story is going to unfold. Others will plan their stories, perhaps down to the most meticulous details, before writing a word of it. There are pros and cons to both approaches.

Winging it
Pros
- The characters 'lead' the story and as a result are often strong, empathic characters that the reader will relate to.
- The writer can get into 'flow' and give their creativity free reign, allowing their intuition to guide their writing. Often, an incredibly tight plot can unfold organically when the writer gets into this zone.

Cons
- A lack of structure can lead the writer into going off on tangents that have little bearing on the story. As a result, extensive editing will need to be done when the writing is finished to uncover the story arc.
- The writer may run out of steam and find they don't know where to go with the story. As a result a potentially great idea may be discarded due to lack of planning.

Planning it
Pros
- A framework to write within means the author knows what's happening and where the writing is going; there's less chance of getting stuck or blocked.

- A strong plan usually results in a strong plot: pacy, gripping, and all loose ends tied up. Any sub-plots and erotic elements are tightly weaved in and integral to the story arc and character development.

Cons

- If a story is highly plot-driven, the characters may be less well-drawn, seemingly caught up in the sequence of events rather than impacting on them.
- If a writer is too rigid in their desire to stick to their plan they may ignore flashes of intuition that would guide them to making beneficial changes.

Personally, and many writers and writing tutors will back me on this, a middle way between the two is best. Have a plan for your story before you write. If you're naturally a bit of a winger and don't want to plot your story scene by scene that's fine, but at the very least have your characters, your basic premise and know what your big question is and how it gets resolved. If you're a rigid planner who writes a 50 page chapter breakdown before getting started, that's fine too, but give your writing permission to breathe; if halfway through your character seems to be unfolding in a different direction, or your intuition tells you a certain scene would work better another way, then listen. Don't make your plan set in stone if you feel there's a better way.

As an example, when writing my first YA romance 'Unconditional' I had a well thought out synopsis and chapter breakdown before I set out to write. I knew my characters and knew what they were doing in each chapter and had a well thought out story arc. However when I got towards the final climactic scene I realised another scene would work better, so that's what I wrote. I didn't change the basic premise; the Big Question of my story was still resolved and the plot was still tight, but this particular change felt more authentic for my characters and more satisfying and dramatic for my reader. In other words, I had a framework to write within and knew what my story arc was and how it unfolded, but if a scene felt like it needed altering as I was writing, then I altered it. Sometimes the best stories take on a life all of their own.

Whatever your individual writing style, if you're writing erotica or a story with erotic elements then I would strongly recommend that you do some planning of these before you start the actual writing to ensure they fit in to and add to your plot.

Of course if you're writing an erotic story then the sex scenes won't just enhance the plot, they may well be the major element of it. That doesn't mean you need to do less planning. As I said in the last chapter there are sadly still many erotic stories that suffer from the lack of any discernible plot. A lot of sex scenes do not an erotic novel make. You still need to know: what is your Big Question? What are the protagonist's motives and goals, and how do they develop during the course of the story? Every sex scene should further this development.

If your story is not an erotic story per se but a different genre that nevertheless you feel would benefit from a strong erotic element, the same principles apply. Each sex scene should tell us something about the characters and should move us further forward in the story.

Keeping the erotic essential: motive, outcomes and development

For your erotic scene to be integral to your plot, it must do at least one of these things

- Cause your character to question him/herself and/or change in some way
- Change the relationship between the characters
- Further the story – come closer to the resolution of the conflict
- Alternatively, throw a spanner in the works by creating more conflict

- Reveal something new about the characters or the story to the reader

For every erotic scene, ask yourself: what are the characters' motives, what is the outcome, and how does it further the story's development? If these have clear answers, then your sex scene is feeding the plot.

Motives

Why are your characters having sex right now? People have all sorts of motives for having sex, from love to curiosity to impending danger to a sense of solace, but whatever the motive, make sure there is one, and your story people aren't just having sex because you've reached a lull in your story. Or just to arouse the reader. Let's go back to our story scenarios from Chapter 3 to look at some possible examples for motives for the first time these characters have sex in the story. Just to recap: we had a woman exploring the different facets of her sexuality in spite of familial and cultural repression, a blossoming romance featuring a tornado chasing commitment-phobe, a rock star becoming embroiled in a gangland war, a detective fighting against time to locate a bomb and a supermodel struggling with the demands of the industry. All of these characters will, in the contexts of their stories, have very different reasons for wanting to have sex. In the erotica story the first sexual encounter will probably be through a sense of curiosity and the longing to explore the sexual self. With the romance, there may be a lot of build up to the initial sex scene between the two characters, and for the commitment-phobe his motives may be conflicted. He desires her, cares about her, but doesn't want to. Perhaps his motive for their first sexual encounter is to get the feelings out of his system?

The first erotic encounter we have with the rock star may be symptomatic of his hedonistic lifestyle and his motive may simply be drug-fuelled desire, at least on the surface. Internally, he's probably conflicted and longing for comfort. The detective, you remember, was getting entangled with the ex he's still in love with, and their first sexual encounter in the story comes about in the midst of a dangerous situation. His motive then may be a mix of wanting to be with the woman he loves one last time, and the instinctive desire for life-affirming sex in the face of possible death. This is a strong human urge that can be exploited for powerful effect when it comes to adding an erotic element to thrillers and action adventure stories.

How about the model? She's probably having sex to feel good about herself, to feel desired. Or perhaps she's acting self-destructively.

If you're struggling to pin down a clear motive, ask yourself – and your character – the following questions:

- What has just happened/is about to happen that could throw sex into the mix?
- What are the underlying tensions?
- What emotions are being experienced? What emotion is your character trying not to experience?
- What's the setting? Is the location particularly enticing?
- What does the character want to change about their current situation?

Outcomes and development

Whatever your characters' motives for getting it on at that precise moment, it's the outcome and subsequent plot and character development that will have the most impact on your story. No matter how compelling your characters' motives or even how hot the actual sex scene, it will seem superfluous if nothing happens in your story as a result. This can be quite subtle – an early erotic encounter for the model gives her a confidence boost that increases throughout the rest of the story – or have all the subtlety of a dropped bomb. Perhaps the detective and his old sweetheart are so engrossed in each other they don't realise the cabin is bugged and get taken hostage as a result, leading to the next point of conflict in the story. If you're writing a romance then the erotic scene – particularly the first encounter – will have a strong outcome for the development of the romance, for good or ill (the strength of his feelings causes the commitment-phobe to do a runner, which leads his love interest into the path of the tornado, for example).

Strangely enough this is often harder to do when writing within the erotica genre, as it's a given that the character is going to be having lots of sex. If you've got, for example, twenty explicit sex scenes in one novella then it's relatively easy to lose track of the story arc and forget to make every encounter count. The impact can be subtle of course; your character doesn't need to have a life-changing experience every ten pages, but every erotic scene should contribute to her development in some way, even if it's as simple as her discovering a new sexual like that she resolves to bring into every further encounter. Or she has the best orgasm of her life and consequentially compares every encounter to that one. In my BDSM story 'Wicked Games' for example, whereas some of the erotic encounters between the couple have dramatic outcomes for their relationships and lives, others show a subtle unfolding of sexual exploration. But there is always an impact.

If you feel it's the right time in your story for a sex scene but you're not sure what the consequences will be for your story and your characters, then ask yourself the following questions:

- How does your character feel about the encounter? Regretful, exhilarated, loved up?
- Have the character's immediate or future plans changed or been altered in any way?
- Does the character want to repeat the experience?
- Has their sexual knowledge or repertoire been expanded or altered?

Whether subtle or explosive, as long as the erotic encounters in your story have clear motivation behind them and a discernable outcome, then you'll be able to ensure they are tightly bound to your overall plot.

Writing Exercise: Recognising motive and outcome

Take three stories that have at least one erotic scene in them, some highlighters and something to take notes on. Read quickly through just the erotic scenes and see if you can discern for yourself what the characters' motives are and what the likely outcome will be. Then, read through the scenes before and after and see if you were right. Determine what the actual motives and outcomes are and how the author has portrayed this. Read ahead a little and see how the encounter has affected the story. Do you think the author has done a good job? Would you do things differently? Do this with each story and then compare and contrast them. Which author has in your opinion used their sex scene most effectively?

Endings and beginnings and avoiding a saggy middle

All stories need a beginning, a middle and an end. That's pretty obvious, you're most likely thinking. However for many writers defining these is a common difficulty, resulting in what's known as a 'saggy middle', and also long-winded beginnings or an anti-climactic ending. Beginnings and endings are the easiest to fix, so let's look at these first.

Your story needs action early on. As early on as possible. If you can't get it on the first page, at least get it into the first chapter. Of course 'action' depends on the type of story you're writing; it could be a car exploding, the heroine first clapping eyes on her hero, a shock announcement at a family gathering, or any number of things. What's important is that you start the story with the starting point, not spend two chapters telling your reader your main character's life story up to that point or describing the setting or taking your protagonist through a typical day in their lives full of every humdrum detail. You may recognise this technique from your school English Literature reading material, particularly the nineteenth century classics, but contemporary readers tend to prefer Dan Brown to Dickens. If nothing much happens until your third chapter, then make it your first. You can weave in necessary background information later on and even make chapter two a flash back (or chapter one a flash forward) but do start your story at the first point of action.

On this note, if you're writing for the explicit erotica genre, should you have a sex scene in the first chapter? I would say yes; perhaps not a full on romp, but at least a taste of what's to come or a peek at the character's sexual fantasies. Ditto if you're writing an erotic romance; have your hero and heroine meeting in the first chapter.

How about your ending? This should be fairly straight-forward, but it can still be tempting for the author to drag on the story for a whole chapter or two after the big climax. Yes, you should tie up all loose ends – unless your deliberately leaving them loose for the sequel – but don't take pages and pages to do so. If necessary you can always add a short epilogue. Bonkbuster queen Jackie Collins tends to do this as her books feature lots of characters and subplots and she always ties up her loose ends. But don't carry on for more than a few pages after the world has been saved, or the dashing rake declares his undying love, or whatever. For example, if you've finally gotten your two main characters in a romance together after a variety of ups and downs, end it quickly. Don't spend a whole extra chapter detailing the reactions of family and friends and what colour serviettes they choose for the wedding. If you drag out ending the story for too long after the final drama, your story will feel anticlimactic, because the reader will be expecting something else of importance to happen, and then, er, it doesn't.

And what about that saggy middle? This is a phrase used to

refer to a story losing its way around the middle of the text, with nothing much going on and the sense of forward motion stalling. Often, this is a case of lack of planning, which is why earlier in this chapter I suggested it's generally preferable to have the bones of your plot worked out beforehand. It's common to conceive of a story's beginning, know your characters and how you want the story to end, but only have a vague idea of what's going to happen in between. Even if you're a fan of winging it, map out a few plot points, road markers if you will, so you're not left with a vague gap that you find yourself struggling to fill.

Another reason for a saggy middle is a lessening of tension and conflict. Remember that story arc: the tension, sexual and otherwise, should keep growing until that big final scene. This may mean adding scenes to your story, but more often you might find that it means culling pages of dialogue, description and scenes that don't really go anywhere to knock your plot into shape.

Whatever you do, don't start filling out the difficult middle part of your book with superfluous sex scenes. For some Ancient Grecian help with this tricky part of plotting, try the following exercise.

Writing Exercise: Aristotle's Three Acts

The Ancient Greek philosopher Aristotle took a great interest in the Grecian tradition of tragedy and comedy plays and noted that they, and stories in general (the Ancient Greeks were fond – very fond – of long epics like the Iliad and the Odyssey) fell into three acts. Aristotle didn't just term these three acts beginning, middle and end, but rather more helpfully he labelled them Set-up, Confrontation and Resolution. Keeping these labels in mind when you're working out your plot will help remind you what each section is supposed to do. The beginning sets the story up, providing the conditions for it to happen; the ending resolves everything, whether satisfactorily or otherwise. As for the middle...notice Aristotle didn't call it the Filler, or the Bit In

Between that exists purely to link a clever set-up to a dramatic resolution. No, he termed it the Confrontation. The part of the plot where the tension mounts, the conflicts grow and the dramas ensue, and your characters develop their relationships with each other. In other words, *it's where the story happens*.

To try this way of planning your story, go back to your notes from the exercise in Chapter Three 'Creating drama and conflict' and pick one of the story outlines you created. From this, create a rough plot. The beginning and end of the story will most likely come to you first, which is fine. Divide your plot into ten segments; these could be pages, scenes, or chapters depending on whether your plot fits a short story length, novella or novel (more of this in Chapter Six). The first two segments are for your Set-up, the last two for your Resolution and the six in between for your Confrontation. This is the meat of your story. Write a few lines for each scene describing what happens. In the middle scenes try and ensure each one builds on the last and the levels of tension are rising, and the characters and their relationships developing, all building up to that final resolution. You've now got a brief but structured synopsis – story outline – that you can use to start writing your story or plotting it further, ensuring that rather than being 'saggy' the middle is in fact the meat of your story.

To give you an example of how this exercise works, I gave it to a writer friend of mine, who came up with the following. From the prompts in the Chapter Three exercise he chose a male tarot card reader with a gambling problem, a fifteenth century courtesan with a stalker, and for the external conflict, the deadly virus outbreak (in keeping with the fifteenth century time frame, this could be bubonic plague). He had the vague idea that the card reader would foresee the coming of the Plague at around the same time as the courtesan sought out his skills to find out who the shadowy figure following her around might be. The story would end with the two characters falling in love and running away to escape the plague, after he saves her from an attempt on her life by the mysterious stalker. After playing around with the Three Acts concept, this is the final plot my friend came up with, which with some tweaking could be turned into a thrilling story – and one with plenty of scope for some scorching scenes.

Set-up
Scene One
The courtesan is hurrying home in her carriage after an assignation with a wealthy benefactor. Entering her London townhouse, she spots a masked man skulking in the shadows and flees inside, confiding to her maid that she fears she's being followed and spied on, recounting recent events. The maid tells her about a new alchemist in the area who reads the cards and is reported to be incredibly skilled. Our heroine resolves to go and see him.
Scene Two
We see our card reader returning home drunk in the early morning from a gambling den, terrified as he has just got himself into serious debt with a notorious villain. He spreads out his cards and gets a vision of the coming plague. He is packing his things ready to flee when our heroine bursts in asking for a reading. Seeing she is both beautiful and distressed our hero agrees, but sees only darkness around her – and also sees her naked in his arms. Thoroughly freaked out, he asks her to leave.

That's the beginning. The writer has started with a good dollop of action and introduced the characters and the conflicts they will be facing, as well as setting the scene for an intimate relationship.

Confrontation
Scene Three
Our heroine returns home to a bouquet of dead flowers and the message she is being watched. We then see a flashback to the

heroine's past where she fled an abusive lover and realise that he has once again found her. Needless to say, she is terrified and cancels her engagements for that night.

Scene Four

Our reluctant hero finds he doesn't want to flee without warning the beautiful courtesan and after making some discreet enquiries tracks her down. He finds her in distress and they both confide their fears in the other, before tumbling into bed and making love, spurred on by their fears and desire for each other.

Scene Five

Our story couple talk further in the morning and he asks the courtesan to flee with him. Although she is tempted she says he can't just go and leave the townspeople to face the coming plague. He then confides what he didn't tell her last night: that he is in serious gambling debt. Furious that he didn't tell her this before they made love, she throws him out.

So here we are halfway through our story and it's not saggy at all; rather we've introduced a sexual relationship between our characters and kept the sexual tension going by having them quarrel and our conflicts and challenges are well underway, with our big questions being: will our characters get it together in time to escape the plague and before either of them get hurt? We also have their separate mysteries/challenges of her stalker and his gambling debt, which have yet to fully unfold.

Scene Six

Our hero is accosted by a masked man in the alley demanding his master's money. He returns home to treat his wounds, conflicted as to what to do as he has feelings for his new lover, when he is struck down with a vision of the plague coming to London via a cargo of infected French linen.

Scene Seven

Meanwhile our courtesan has attended the gambling den with the intention of locating the hero's creditor and seducing him in an attempt to find a way to call him off her newfound love.

Instead, she finds herself winning a large amount of money from her besotted co-gamblers. She rushes to our hero and finds him in distress after his vision. After deciding to do their best to prevent the cargo from landing, and she reveals she has the money to help him, they again go to bed and have sex.

Scene Eight

In the morning they confess their developing feeling for each other and make tender love. Questioning him about his injuries she realises his assailant is none other than her ex-lover who has also been harassing her. Our hero is full of protectiveness and intent on finding him but the young courtesan convinces him they must stop the infected cargo first. On their way to the docks in the carriage they learn the cargo has just landed.

So there we are, we've reached the Resolution and the pace hasn't let up once. The conflict has reached boiling point and two big questions need to be resolved: can our lovers stop the plague reaching London and can they escape the villain intent on harming the courtesan?

Why don't you have a go at writing your own final scenes? Also, look over the rest of the plot. Can you identify any weaknesses and if so how would you change them? Look at where the sex scenes are; do they add to the story with clear motives and outcomes? Could you spice the story up to make it hotter? Then do the same with your own story outlines.

Chapter Overview

- Your protagonist's main goals and motivations are what drive your plot.
- Some authors plot their story down to the last detail before writing, others 'wing it'. There are pros and cons to both, but a middle way between the two is most effective.
- When plotting your sex scenes, ask yourself questions

about how they impact on your story to ensure they are integral to the plot.

- What are your character's motives for having sex in this particular place and time?
- What will be the outcome of this erotic encounter and how will it further the development of your characters and their story?
- Look at other authors' work to see how they plot their erotic scenes.
- Your story needs a defined beginning, middle and end.
- The beginning should include action, not just background and character sketches.
- Wrap up the story quickly after the final dramatic scene, but be sure to tie up any loose ends.
- Writers often suffer from 'saggy middle' syndrome where the story peters out and loses pace halfway through. This is generally due to lack of planning and/or a lessening instead of intensifying of drama and conflict.
- In fact the middle should be the meat of your story, where the conflict rises and the characters are clearly growing and developing as the story picks up pace towards the ending. Good plotting helps with this.
- Aristotle defined the 'three acts' of story as Set-up, Confrontation and Resolution. Try the writing exercise for an in-depth look at using this framework to plot your story.

So now finally, we come to the crux of the matter. You know what makes your characters tick and you've worked those sizzling erotic scenes into your plot. Now it's time to look at how to craft those sexy scenes for maximum arousal and engagement with the reader. Yup, it's time to talk dirty.

Chapter Five

Getting Down and Dirty

In this chapter we're going to focus on the sex scenes themselves. I've left this until near the end of the guide because sexy stories, like any story, are all about the characters, the conflict and the plot. Now we've got those in place, we can have a look at the nuts and bolts of writing those sex scenes. And let's not forget, they need to be *sexy*. Before you try any of the exercises or tips in this chapter, go back and read your notes from the exercise at the end of the Introduction 'How do you define erotic?'

For your sex scenes to work for your story they need to be both arousing, well written and real. Let's get the practicalities out of the way first.

Creating realistic sex scenes

It doesn't matter how hot your sex scenes are if they're so unbelievable the reader is rolling their eyes with disbelief. Here a few common mistakes

- The characters have far superior sexual skills to the rest of the human race (the man is so well-endowed it's a wonder he can walk and as well as being able to orgasm five times himself in one night – with no rest in between – he makes the heroine climax ten times through straight intercourse alone). Yes, you're writing fantasy, but it needs to be a fantasy the reader can relate to.
- Unrealistic setting. In the middle of the park for example, with no mention of passers-by or stray dogs. That's not to say you can't take your characters out of the bedroom – please do – but make sure you cover all eventualities.
- The characters suddenly stop and have sex at the most

ridiculous of times. Yes, I know I stressed that if you're writing a thriller then dangerous situations can provide a great motive for some urgent life-affirming sex, but do make sure your characters aren't so carried away they start being 'too stupid to live'. Stopping in the middle of running away from kidnappers to have a quick romp, for example. A sense of danger is one thing, immediate danger is another.

- Putting your characters into physically impossible positions. It's easily done, when writing an adventurous sex scene, to forget where you originally put various limbs and to end up describing a scene that is in fact anatomically impossible. I experienced this myself writing an erotic scene using a sex swing. I became quite engrossed in this scene and believed it was the hottest in the whole story. I only realised I had overlooked the mechanics of it when my editor kindly asked when the hero had sprouted a third arm! I also spotted a similar mistake myself in a self-published lesbian erotica story where one character, all at the same time, had the fingers of one hand in her lover's mouth, the other hand touching her intimately, and a mysterious third hand taking her weight on a nearby piece of furniture. The reader will notice; after all your aim is to create the scenario in their mind's eye and mistakes of this kind will be spotted and will quite probably jar the reader out of the story.

As you can see, there are a few practicalities you need to bear in mind, and as long as we as authors keep an eye on these things the reader can allow themselves to be swept into the heat of the moment. You can certainly be experimental with your sex scenes, just cast a keen eye over them for any of the inconsistencies mentioned above. If you're writing a story with sci-fi, futuristic or paranormal elements you have more leeway when it comes to sexual performance – who's to say your shape shifter or half-alien hero can't perform five times a night? – but do ensure your reader understands that this is due to the elements of your alternative world or more than human characters.

Sensuality

We spoke about using sensual details to add to sexual tension, and they work in the same way to add to the heat of your sex scene. A common complaint about unsatisfactory erotic scenes is that they are either too physical bodily orientated, reading like a biology textbook, or that they describe the characters' feelings without any details of what they are actually doing. Adding sensual detail can transform and add heat to both of these approaches. For example,

John turned Jane over and kissed her breasts and then her thighs isn't very sexy, but add some sensory experience and we have *John pulled Jane into him, feeling the heat of her skin, then lowered his lips to the pink tips of her breasts, before trailing rough lips down her body to the softness of her thighs* which is much more evocative.

Or if we look at the alternative problem of writing that isn't physical enough:

Jane was giddy with exhilaration and full of a sweet sharp joy as John showered her body with love is romantic, but tells us nothing about what they're doing and isn't erotic, not by today's standards in any case. Replace some of the emotion with sensory detail however and the heat level instantly rises. *Jane felt giddy as she tipped her head back and arched her body towards John, his lips on the curve of her breasts filling her with a sweet, sharp pleasure low in her belly. His lips traced a burning line down to her thighs and he looked up at her with both love and heat in his eyes as he nibbled her soft flesh.* Here we still have the emotion required for a more traditional romance, but the image is much more erotic.

Sensuality doesn't just apply to what the characters are doing to each other. You can apply sensory detail to what's going on around them also to add to the eroticism of the scene. If they're having sex outside in the sun for example make use of the heat on their skin, the smell of fresh cut grass and the bright blue of the sky. If they're in the shower, how does that water feel across their bodies? If your characters are in bed, the smell of clean linen or the feel of crisp sheets all add to the scene. Bring all of the five senses into play.

Writing Exercise: Using the Five Senses

Look again at the notes you made for the 'How do you define erotic?' exercise and circle any mention of sense impressions. Brainstorm any sensations you find erotic. For example;

Sight
The curve of a strong buttock; long hair falling down a back; moisture on skin; sparkling eyes; smooth lines; the intricate patterns of fishnet against skin...

Smell
Fresh flowers; musk; the tang of sweat; clean linen; engine oil; hot tarmac; baking bread....

Taste
Skin; melted chocolate; champagne on the tongue; wine in a lover's mouth....

Sound
A low growl or soft moan from a lover; the sound of bodies coming together; a deep throbbing bass; thunder in the distance...

Touch
Silk sheets; rough calloused palms; a tongue-tip; sun, wind or rain on skin; a wool rug; rope....

Now write a few sentences using sense details for an erotic scene involving a couple making love in a shower. Then try again for a couple indulging in hard core BDSM play. Sensuality doesn't necessarily mean 'soft'. Whatever your characters are getting up to, give your reader a glimpse of what they are seeing, feeling, hearing, tasting and smelling and you will breathe life into your erotic encounters.

Erotic language and creating your own glossary

One of the hardest problems for writers wrestling with erotic scenes, especially those fairly new to this, is *what to call things*? Specifically, body parts. Personally I prefer to call a spade a spade. Or a cock, a cock. It's certainly preferable to euphemisms such as 'quivering manhood' (though these may have a place in historical settings where the characters would have used those terms), overly anatomical terms (she flicked his frenulum) or the names you used to use as a child. No rubbing of fairies or foofies, it's patronising and even slightly disturbing. Equally, most readers will be turned off or in fits of giggles if you start talking about his manly weapon or the delicate, dewy petals of her lady garden.

Having said that, if you're writing for a specific heat level or publisher, or in a genre not usually associated with overtly explicit scenes, straight to the point words such as 'cock' and 'pussy' may be deemed as too pornographic or even offensive to the reader. Which leaves the writer in a bit of a bind.

There are two approaches to this. Firstly, use words that are direct but not too explicit or anatomical. Here a few ideas:

Shaft (penis)
Head (of penis)
Sac (testicles)
Cleft (vagina or vulva)
Nub (clitoris)

Use these words in a direct manner without adding flowery adjectives – so no tumescent shafts or pearly nubs – and you can't go too far wrong. If you don't like these words, find some of your own. Read authors experienced at writing sex scenes – especially within your chosen genre – and make notes of similar words they use that work for you. Keep a little notebook to build up your own erotic vocabulary, and you'll soon have a list of words and phrases to use when you want to change the heat levels or substitute one word for another simply to avoid repetition. 'Shaft' instead of 'cock' for example.

There's also another approach. Don't name the genitals at all. Before you think this is going to be impossible if the scene you intend to write is quite explicit, think again. Consider the sentence *he slid inside her, masking her gasp*. It's explicit, to the point, and quite sexy. It can be made hotter with the inclusion of sensory details, or more romantic by mentioning what emotions the characters are experiencing. Yet no names have been used, because we don't need them. We know exactly what he is sliding where. Similar expressions would be

He entered her
She rode his body
She caressed his length
He pushed his fingers into her slowly
As he tasted her, he looked up wickedly from between her thighs.

Again, play around with this. Try some phrases of your own, see how other authors do it, and record the phrases you like. Then have a go at writing a few sentences with each. You'll have the outline of a steamy scene before you know it.

Going all the way vs. going too far

How hot is too hot? It depends on your target audience, the genre requirements and your own comfort levels. Don't try writing explicit BDSM if it makes you cringe, as this will come across. Equally, if you feel your scene is too tame, don't be scared to spice it up a little.

As always, read. All genres have their own expectations that come with them and it's up to you if you choose to write safely within them or skate close to the edge. Read authors in your genre that you admire and take note of their self-defined boundaries. Also, listen to your own story and your characters and take a look at the setting. A sex scene involving a man, woman and sex toy might work perfectly for our rock star story, but less well for the scene between the detective and his ex. She may well, as a modern woman, own a vibrator but is she really likely to be carrying it around in her handbag while fleeing terrorists? As always, consider your plot. Ditto with your genre. If your novel has a historical setting, consider the social mores of the time. Upper class ladies in Regency England are highly unlikely to have been engaging in same sex threesomes, but go back to pagan Rome and you might be on to something. If your thriller has an action packed plot then anything but the simplest of sex scenes may be unnecessary and distracting. Don't be afraid to include purely 'vanilla' (no toys, props, dressing up or Kama Sutra positions) sex. It can be surprisingly hot. A long, slow afternoon in bed or a passionate quickie outside, if well written, is often all your reader needs and as a general guideline if you're writing in a genre other than erotica or hot erotic romance then keeping it simple is usually best.

If you are writing erotica or erotic romance, there are clear categories for heat levels and explicit scenarios within most sub-genres, so your story will fit in somewhere but as above, think about your plot and characters. Rather than, say, throwing in an anal sex or BDSM scene because you're writing for the extreme erotic romance end, when it doesn't feel in keeping with your characters or where they are in the story. BDSM in particular tends to involve a whole lifestyle so if it's not already part of your plot then the hero isn't likely to suddenly whip out the cable ties and nipple clamps.

In other words then, the only restrictions on your erotic scenes are those imposed by your characters and your story, and if you've explored your story people and plotted ahead, these will speak for themselves.

The list of things you absolutely can't write in any category or genre is fairly obvious, but you'll still find them stated clearly in all publisher's guidelines. Which does make you wonder how many editors still receive manuscripts of this kind. These lists are usually along the lines of

- No incest
- No rape
- No forced BDSM
- No body waste fluids (although one or two mainstream erotica novels featuring 'golden showers' have recently hit the headlines)
- No minors
- No necrophilia (vampires and even possibly zombies are fine)
- No bestiality (werewolves etc are fine, but not when they're in animal form)

Of course, topics such as rape and incest do come up in commercial fiction, as well as some of the other nasties, but as harrowing scenes in crime and horror novels, not as erotic encounters intended to arouse. Thankfully I'm pretty sure that for the majority of us, this goes without saying.

How not to do it – the Bad Sex Award

Every year in the UK the Literary Review gives out its Bad Sex in Fiction award. To give you a few examples, here are a few (anonymous) snippets from winners and runners-up in recent years.

I was immersed in the slush of her moist meat.

'She began to gasp. "Oh dear, oh my dear, oh my dear dear God, oh sugar!"'

The bed shook and bounced and walked tiny fractions across the moving floor.

His manhood had swelled to its fullness and strove for release.

A freshly made ear and a freshly made vagina look very much alike.

...these sorts of gyrations and five-sense choreographies...

Believe it or not these phrases are all from best-selling authors in genres ranging from literary, romance, thriller and mystery.

What do you think?

Connecting with the reader and getting in the mood

Your erotic scenes should be strong if you've followed the advice in this guide, and having well-drawn, empathic characters, a tight plot full of rising tension and sensual yet direct sex talk will all engage your reader in the story. There's one last point I'd like to consider, although it's hard to define and impossible to teach, and that's your connection to the reader.

Often, when we read a scene that evokes a particular emotion in us, although that may be because of our own subjective experience, it's also in large part down to the emotions the author poured into the page. If you feel tearful when you're writing a sad scene for example, then there's a strong chance your reader will too. No matter how sharp and skilful your writing, on the other hand, if you are bored by your story this will communicate itself through to your audience. Yes, it's important to have good characterisation and plot and use the right language and description but you should be able to feel your story too. The best writers are often those who are passionate about their work, and if you can't get passionate about an erotic scene, when can you?

In short, it's okay to be slightly aroused yourself when writing your erotic scenes, or later when you read them back through. In fact, it's a very good sign. That's the effect you're trying to create, after all.

So when you sit down to write your erotic scenes, it's a good idea to 'get yourself in the mood'. Relax, and spoil your senses. I've heard of lots of writers who have little rituals or certain songs they like to listen to or aromatherapy oils they burn to evoke certain moods etc. and I'm no different. If I'm in the middle of writing an erotic romance I'll be reading lots of it, watching romantic and sexy films and listening to lots of sultry R'n' B. When I sit down to write I'll have a playlist of sexy songs on repeat in the background, and perhaps even a scented candle burning. It works for me. Only you can find what works for you.

Writing Exercise: Write your own sex scene using memory

Now you're going to have a go at writing a full length sex scene, using the advice in this chapter. I don't want you to have to do too much thinking about who your characters are, what you're doing and why for this exercise so to ensure that your erotic scene already has developed characters and a plot, we're going to use a real memory. Yours. Pick a favourite past erotic encounter; it can be anything you choose as long as it's a good memory, and turn it into a sex scene. Of course you may find yourself tweaking certain details and you could even tailor it to fit in the plot of a current story you are writing or planning, but in terms of the sexual content, use your memory. If you want to detach from it a little, write in the third-person rather than the first.

Use some of the words and phrases from your own erotic glossary or my suggestions that you like and think about where and when you can add sensory detail to create an evocative picture. Let yourself be immersed in the memories as you write.

Go.

Read over it a few days later and see how you feel and if there are any parts you would change. Then try writing a fictional sex scene for your plot structure from the exercise at the end of Chapter Four.

Chapter Overview

- Your erotic scenes need to be realistic to engage the reader – no super marathons or impossible feats of flexibility.
- Where are you setting your scene? Cover any possible practicalities such as making it clear your characters are secluded if outside etc.
- If you're writing a thriller or horror, make sure your characters are safe for the moment before they drop everything and have sex.
- Use sensory detail to spice up both prose that is too stilted or too flowery and emotional. Where possible include all five senses.
- Brainstorm some sensual images and use them to craft a few sexy sentences as shown in the writing exercise.
- Keep erotic language direct and simple.
- You can write explicitly without using explicit words if they're inappropriate for your genre – see the examples.
- Take notes of words and phrases you like and create your own erotic glossary you can draw from.
- Research the boundaries of your genre to see how far you can push sexual boundaries.
- Let the sexual activities be determined by your characters and your story.
- Try not to win the Bad Sex Award – see examples – but be reassured by the fact that even bestselling authors fall foul of this.
- If you find your scenes arousing, chances are your reader will too.

- Get yourself in the mood for writing erotic scenes with writing aids and rituals such as music or scents.
- Use an erotic memory to craft a compelling erotic scene.
- Then try a fictional one. Good luck!

You're now well on your way to crafting your own erotic stories and scenes. Continue to research, and read, and above all, write! In the final section of this guide I'll offer some tips and exercises towards publication if that's your goal, and a few online resources to help you on your way.

From Pitch to Publication

This is a writing guide, rather than a how to get published guide, but nevertheless if you spend time writing and honing your craft and produce work you are proud of, you're likely to want to share it. Not all writers are lucky enough to make a full-time living out of their writing, but regardless of money and bestseller lists, having your work out there and being enjoyed by readers is a reward in itself. So here are a few final thoughts and things for you to try if you want to see your work in print.

Research and queries

Do your research. If you are looking to have a novel traditionally published, it's advisable to have an agent. Although smaller publishers will often accept queries and proposals directly from a new author, if you have an agent it's an indication to the publisher that your work has already been deemed as worth a punt by someone in the know. Agents act as filters, if you like.

Whatever you decide on this score, do your research. Ensure that the agent or publisher you are approaching is a good fit for your work – don't offer your gory horror to an agent specialising in warm family sagas, for example – and follow their submission guidelines. Read writing magazines, make Google your friend, and get yourself a copy of the highly recommended Writers and Artists Handbook, published by Bloomsbury and updated with a new edition every year. It lists every resource an aspiring writer or illustrator could ever need, from listings of agents, publishers and magazines to writing competitions and groups, as well as exclusive articles from agents, editors and bestselling authors. On all aspects of writing from the creative to the financial.

Make a list of agents and/or publishers that you think may be interested in your work and start querying them. Check whether they prefer initial contact by email or post.

Always start with a query letter before you send your manuscript and synopsis (in depth outline of the story). If they like the sound of your manuscript they will ask to see it, whereas if you just send along your manuscript without being asked (known as 'unsolicited') there's a strong chance it will be deleted without ever being looked at. Your query letter then is absolutely crucial as it's your first point of contact with your future agent and or publisher.

Here are a few dos and don'ts, as well as a winning example.

Do

- Be polite and formal (if you're querying by email still set it out as a letter. No smiley faces or text speak).
- Check you have names correct and you're addressing the right person in the relevant department.
- Provide a brief CV particularly of your writing history and any background that's relevant to your work.
- Mention any contacts within the industry who are willing to provide endorsements.
- Give a succinct, interesting summary of your work.
- Mention the intended audience and any competing works or similar authors. The first thing the agent or publisher will want to know is whether there's a market for it.
- Be patient. It may take a few months before you get a response.
- Be resilient. Even the best writers get dozens of rejections. Try the next name on your list.

Don't

- Give them your entire life story.
- Be too arrogant 'I expect this book to be in huge demand so you would do well to take the chance I'm offering you to represent it'.

- Be too humble 'it's probably not very good and you'll hate it but I'd appreciate you having a look'.
- Expect detailed feedback if it's a no. These are busy people.
- Mention how your family and friends think it's wonderful. Of course they do.
- Slag off other authors, agents or publishers.
- Keep sending follow-up e-mails every few days. Agents and publishers receive hundreds of queries and it takes a while to get through them all. If you keep cluttering up their inbox, you will be deleted. Having said that, if you haven't heard anything after a few months, a very polite e-mail is fine.

Writing Exercise: Write a query letter

An agent friend of mine shared with me the following query letter that she confessed really impressed her, to the point that she knew she would be signing up this author even before she read the work (she did). Some details have been left out, but here are is the basic letter as an example of how to write a successful query.

Dear .....

I am writing to query if you would be interested in my manuscript .... My work is an explicit and dramatic erotic novel featuring a fashion model who embarks on a period of sexual exploration. It gives a fictional yet realistic view into the sometimes fun, sometimes frightening, and often bizarre world of fashion modelling and the inevitable problems and struggles that arise. It is both an erotic and a cautionary tale, incorporating an evocative love story, culminating in a – for now at least – true happy ending.

I firmly believe there is a wide market for this book, as this genre has proved very popular in recent years. However, I believe I have a story to tell that is fresh and exciting, giving the reader a glimpse into an otherwise unknown world, and also tapping into the thirst for celebrity gossip and romance. Therefore I feel there would be a wide readership for this book; being essentially a redemption story with a 'good girl gone bad' theme and a romantic sub-story it would appeal to female readers in general; also the erotic content is timely in the wake of recent interest in 'mummy porn'; this is a look at the real thing. The book would also contribute to current debates concerning the mainstreaming of the porn industry into our culture, as outlined for example in Natasha Walters 'Living Dolls'. I also have a small yet growing social media platform and would be able to promote this work through my own pages and blogs.

I have also written short erotic fiction, forthcoming in anthologies later this year. I also write articles and poetry and contribute on a regular basis to …. magazine.

I hope my proposal will be of some interest to you and I wonder if you would be happy for me to send a synopsis and sample chapters to you, or the full manuscript, by post or e-mail?

Thanking you for your consideration.

This was a successful query letter for a number of reasons. It was polite and informative yet direct and clear. The author summed up her work and the target audience, and why she believed it would have appeal. She gave relevant details about her writing history as well as indicated she would take steps to promote herself and her work – always a plus.

Using the above letter as a template, write a sample query letter for your current or planned story.

Publishing and self-publishing

Thanks to the advent of e-books and e-readers such as the astronomically popular Kindle, and self-publishers offering print-on-demand books, sometimes for royalty share rather than the author having to pay any money upfront, it has never been easier to self-publish. Many authors are going down this route, especially as the big traditional publishing houses take on fewer and fewer new authors and pay increasingly smaller advances – if any.

The good news is that if you want to get your work out there, you can. The bad news is that it's just as difficult to get your work noticed in an increasingly over-saturated market that is, sadly, full of some very poor writing. Of course, there are great writers too, but lack of quality control means readers often have to sift through a lot of badly edited work to find the good stuff.

Of course, if your aim is just to get your work out there then the new self-publishing opportunities will be great for you and erotica in particular is booming in this market, especially when it comes to e-books.

If you are happy to share your work for free in exchange for reader feedback and a supportive writing community there are online platforms such as Wattpad (for any genre) and Lush Stories (for erotica). Teenage author Beth Reekles was signed by Random House in 2012 for a three book deal after her YA novel *The Kissing Booth* attracted thousands of fans on Wattpad. Such stories are ultra rare, but they happen.

The short story market

As far as most genres are concerned, the short story market – especially in print – is non-existent. For erotic stories however, this is far from the case. Erotica and romance publishers regularly run submission calls for themed short stories and novellas for inclusion in anthologies. If you're looking to write within this genre, this is a great way to start. See Resources for further information.

Even if you are a writer in another genre looking to write better erotic scenes, writing erotic short stories can really hone your skills and give you some great practice. There are smaller erotica publishers who regularly ask for stories with paranormal themes, sci-fi themes, historical settings, murder mysteries... even steampunk and horror; the list is endless. Whatever your preferred genre you will find an erotica publisher looking for themed short stories with elements of that genre. Again, see Resources.

The erotic e-market

The digital market for erotica and romance is booming, both with authors self-publishing and erotic presses releasing ranges of e-book imprints. Fifty Shades started as online fan fiction, after all. As with the short story market there are themes and genres to suit everyone. I've listed the major imprints in Resources. Check out their websites and read widely within your preferred genre.

Writing Exercise: Write your Mission Statement

Where do you want your writing to go? Ask yourself this honestly and don't be afraid to dream big. Then write down your mission statement as a third person author bio. Make it big, bold and colourful and put it somewhere you can look at it every single day, or whenever you're feeling despondent about your latest rejection. The key is to write it *as if it has already happened*. Go on, don't be shy. Here's an example.

> *John Smith won the prestigious Man Booker Prize this year for his latest in bestselling crime series The Cartman Files. One of the world's most popular writers, as well as one of the most prolific, he began his career with the New York Times bestseller Murder One.*

If such blatant positive thinking makes you sneer, do it anyway. Then take some realistic goals and break them down into baby steps. And remember, even JK Rowling was rejected.

I'd like to leave you with the following quotes:

> *'The universe is change; our life is what our thoughts make it.'*
> Marcus Aurelius

'A writer must write if he is to be at peace with himself. What one can be, one must be.'
Abraham Maslow

And this from me:

'I do not believe that faith can move mountains. But I do know it makes them easier to climb.'

Resources

General – Books

The Writers and Artists Handbook 2014 (Bloomsbury 2013)

The Writers and Artists Guide to How to Write (Harry Bingham, Bloomsbury 2012)

The Writers and Artists Guide to Getting Published (Harry Bingham, Bloomsbury 2012)

www.writersandartists.co.uk

The Positively Productive Writer (Simon Whaley, Compass Books, 2012)

Handy Hints for Writers (Lynne Hackles, Compass Books, 2013)

How to Write a Romance Novel (Susan Palmquist, Compass Books, 2013)

Wicked Games (Kelly Lawrence, Black Lace Books, 2013)

General – Online

www.thewritingplatform.com

www.eroticareaders-writers.com – lists of publishers and submission calls

www.wattpad.com

www.createspace.com – self-publishing via ebooks and print on demand

www.lulu.com – print on demand, no upfront fees

Erotica Presses and Publishers

Black Lace Books (a division of Ebury Publishing, Random House UK) – www.blacklace.co.uk

Circlet Press – Erotic Sci-Fi and Fantasy www.circlet.com

Cleis Press (print) – www.cleispress.com

Ellora's Cave – www.ellorascave.com

Harlequin and Harlequin Mills and Boon – all genres and heat levels – www.harlequin.com

Mischief Books (an imprint of Avon/HarperCollins) – www.mischiefbooks.com

Xcite Books (an imprint of Accent Press) – www.xcitesexystories.com

You can contact the author at www.michellekellylawrence.weebly.com and on Twitter @lotuswriter

About The Author

Kelly has been writing since she was able to pick up a pen and wrote her first novel, an historical romance about Anne Boleyn, at the tender age of twelve; it consists of 200 notebook pages tied together with string and still takes pride of place in her grandmother's display cabinet. She was married at eighteen and divorced at twenty-one, and graduated with first class honours from Warwick University in the meantime. After seven years as a literacy teacher she now writes full time. 'Wicked Games' was her first book, a true-life erotic memoir that she hopes will scandalise the locals in the beautiful village she now lives in, in the heart of the Derbyshire Dales. Her first romance for Harlequin Mills and Boon 'The Virgin Courtesan' is published in October 2013 and she also writes New Adult romance. She lives with her wonderful and long-suffering partner and has recently become a practicing Buddhist, mainly because it keeps her sane, and writes regularly about this at www.meditatelikeagirl.com.

**COMPASS
BOOKS**

Compass Books focuses on practical and informative 'how-to' books for writers. Written by experienced authors who also have extensive experience of tutoring at the most popular creative writing workshops, the books offer an insight into the more specialised niches of the publishing game.